Blind Spots

Blind Spots

Why We Fail to Do What's Right
and What to Do about It

Max H. Bazerman
Ann E. Tenbrunsel

Princeton University Press

Princeton and Oxford

Library of Congress Cataloging-in-Publication Data

Bazerman, Max H.
    Blind spots : why we fail to do what's right and what to do about it / Max H. Bazerman,
Ann E. Tenbrunsel.
        p. cm.
    Includes bibliographical references and index.
    ISBN 978-0-691-14750-5 (cloth : alk. paper)   1. Business ethics.   2. Corporate culture.
3. Decision making—Social aspects.   I. Tenbrunsel, Ann E.   II. Title.
    HF5387.B39 2011
    174′.4—dc22   2010046640

British Library Cataloging-in-Publication Data is available

This book has been composed in Scala and Avenir

Printed on acid-free paper ∞

Printed in the United States of America

10 9 8 7 6 5 4 3 2 1

This book is dedicated to Dave Messick, whose ideas inspired us to study behavioral ethics, even before behavioral ethics had a name.

Contents

Acknowledgments

We have been working on this book for the last two decades—though we didn't know this for much of the time. In 1991, Ann entered the doctoral program at Northwestern University's Kellogg School of Management and spent much of her time there doing some of the early research that brought psychology into the realm of business ethics. Central to this work was Ann's collaboration with David Messick, who arrived at about the same time, as the first Kaplan Distinguished Professor of Ethics at Kellogg. Their work examined ethical fading, or the tendency for otherwise ethical people to make unethical decisions because the ethical implications have faded from their decisions. Max connected with Ann and Dave on some of this research, but was largely an observer and fan of this work.

In 2000, Max joined the Harvard University faculty and started conducting research with new colleagues Mahzarin Banaji and Dolly Chugh on what we called bounded ethicality, or the systematic ways in which people engage in unethical behavior without their own awareness. The ideas that resulted from this collaboration, together with those from Dave and Ann's collaboration, proliferate throughout this book.

At about the same time, Enron collapsed, and organizations and business schools were pushed to do something about the erosion of ethics in society. Consequently, the field of business ethics started to shift in ways that are described throughout our book. One core shift was the development of the field of behavioral ethics, which focuses on the psychology of how real people act in ethical contexts. Interest in behavioral ethics has grown exponentially over the past decade, and this burst of interest prompted us to combine our view of behavioral ethics in this book.

Our work on ethics has been affected by our interactions and collaborations with many scholars. Some of these scholars include Modupe Akinola, Mahzarin Banaji, Iris Bohnet, Art Brief, Daylian Cain, Eugene

Caruso, Suzanne Chan-Serafin, Dolly Chugh, Luke Coffman, John Darley, David de Cremer, Tina Diekmann, Nick Epley, Francesca Gino, Josh Greene, Jennifer Jordan, Karim Kassam, Rod Kramer, Marijke Leliveld, George Loewenstein, Kathleen McGinn, David Messick, Katy Milkman, Celia Moore, Don Moore, Charles Naquin, Maggie Neale, Greg Northcraft, Neeru Paharia, Madan Pillutla, Todd Rogers, Lisa Shu, Kristin Smith-Crowe, Phil Tetlock, Chia-Jung Tsay, Elizabeth Umphress, Erik van Dijk, Kimberly Wade-Benzoni, and other coauthors and friends whom we will be embarrassed for forgetting later.

The quality and presentation of the ideas in this book was dramatically affected by a number of people. Art Brief, Dolly Chugh, Kristina Diekmann, Francesca Gino, Josh Greene, Dave Messick, Madan Pillutla, Todd Rogers, and Kristin Smith-Crowe read and provided insightful feedback on an earlier draft of the manuscript. The book is far better as a result. We also benefited from fantastic editorial help. Katie Shonk, Max's longtime research assistant, coauthor, and editor, made each and every sentence better, as she always does (if you like the writing, get a copy of Katie's new novel, *Happy Now?*). Her help was invaluable. Sarah Oliver-Johnson provided the wonderful illustrations of the trolley and footbridge problems. Ranjan Ahuja proofread, error-checked, and generally fixed what needed to be fixed. Our editors at Princeton University Press, Eric Schwartz, Beth Clevenger, and Janie Chan, provided excellent guidance throughout and added great value. Finally, we thank our families—Max's wife, Marla; Ann's husband, Dante; her children, Dante, Lina, and Michel; and her dad, Don—for their support as we wrote the book.

Blind Spots

Chapter 1

The Gap between Intended and Actual Ethical Behavior

> For some reason I can't explain, I know St. Peter won't call my name.
> —"Viva La Vida," Coldplay

How ethical do you think you are compared to other readers of this book? On a scale of 0 to 100, rate yourself relative to the other readers. If you believe you are the most ethical person in this group, give yourself a score of 100. If you think you're the least ethical person in this group, give yourself a score of 0. If you are average, give yourself a score of 50. Now, if you are part of an organization, also rate your organization: On a scale of 0 to 100, how ethical is it compared to other organizations?

How did you and your organization do? If you're like most of the people we've asked, each of your scores is higher than 50. If we averaged the scores of those reading this book, we guess that it would probably be around 75. Yet that can't actually be the case; as we told you, the average score would have to be 50. Some of you must be overestimating your ethicality relative to others.[1] It's likely that most of us overestimate our ethicality at one point or another. In effect, we are unaware of the gap between how ethical we think we are and how ethical we truly are.

This book aims to alert you to your ethical blind spots so that you are aware of that gap—the gap between who you want to be and the person you actually are. In addition, by clearing away your organizational and societal blind spots, you will be able to close the gap between the organization you actually belong to and your ideal organization. This, in turn, will help us all to narrow the gap between the society we want to live in and the one in which we find ourselves. Drawing on the burgeoning field of behavioral ethics, which examines how and why people behave the way they do in the face of ethical dilemmas, we will make you aware of your ethical blind spots and suggest ways to remove them.

Behavioral Ethics: A New Way of Understanding Unethical Behavior

Consider these two opinions regarding responsibility for the financial crisis that began in 2008:

> This recession was not caused by a normal downturn in the business cycle. It was caused by a perfect storm of irresponsibility and poor decision-making that stretched from Wall Street to Washington to Main Street.
> —President Barack Obama

> The mistakes were systemic—the product of the nature of the banking business in an environment shaped by low interest rates and deregulation rather than the antics of crooks and fools.
> —Richard Posner

Same financial crisis, two different explanations from two famous citizens. The first blames the "bad boys" who operated in our financial system, the second the system in which those bad boys operated. Who's right? Both are—but, even if combined, both opinions are incomplete.

Did some greedy, ill-intentioned individuals contribute to the crisis? Absolutely! As President Obama notes, self-interested actors engaged in clearly illegal behavior that helped bring about the crisis, and these criminals should be sent to jail. Was the financial system destined to produce such behavior? Again, absolutely! Many of our institutions, laws, and regulations are in serious need of reform. Do these two explanations, even when combined, fully explain the financial crisis? Absolutely not!

Missing from these analyses are the thousands of people who were culpably ignorant, engaged in what they thought were seemingly harmless behaviors without consciously recognizing they were doing anything wrong: the mortgage lenders who only vaguely understood that buyers couldn't afford the homes they wanted, the analysts who created mortgage-backed securities without understanding the ripple effect of such a product, the traders who sold the securities without grasping their complexity, the bankers who lent too much, and the regulators biased by the lobbying efforts and campaign donations of investment banks. The crisis also involves the multitude of people who were aware of the unethical behavior of others, yet did little or nothing in response, assuming perhaps that "someone smarter than them understood how it all worked," as *BusinessWeek* speculated.[2]

Numerous scandals that have occurred in the new millennium have damaged our confidence in our businesses and our leaders. Under pressure to become more ethical, organizations and financial institutions have undertaken efforts aimed at improving and enforcing ethical behavior within their walls. They have spent millions of dollars on corporate codes of conduct, value-based mission statements, ethical ombudsmen, and ethical training, to name just a few types of ethics and compliance management strategies. Other efforts are more regulatory in nature, including the Sarbanes-Oxley Act passed by the U.S. Congress; changes to the rules that determine how the New York Stock Exchange governs its member firms; and changes in how individual corporations articulate and communicate their ethical standards to their employees, monitor employees' behavior, and punish deviance.

While we support efforts to encourage more ethical decisions within organizations, the results of these efforts have been decidedly mixed. One influential study of diversity programs even found that creating diversity programs—an organizational attempt to "do the right thing"—has a *negative* impact on the subsequent diversity of organizations.[3] Moreover, such interventions are nothing new. Many similar changes have been made in the past to address ethical indiscretions. Despite these expensive interventions, new ethical scandals continue to emerge.

Similarly, ethics programs have grown at a rapid rate at business schools across the globe, and ratings of business schools now often explicitly assess the prevalence of ethics training in the curriculum. Yet the effects of such ethics training are arguably short-lived, and MBA honor codes, usually part of the educational process, have in some cases been proven to produce no discernible improvement in ethical behavior. In fact, according to a 2008 survey conducted by the Aspen Institute, MBA students feel *less* prepared to deal with value conflicts the longer they are in school.[4]

Could the financial crisis have been solved by giving all individuals involved more ethics training? If the training resembled that which has historically and is currently being used, the answer to that question is no. Ethics interventions have failed and will continue to fail because they are predicated on a false assumption: that individuals recognize an ethical dilemma when it is presented to them. Ethics training presumes that emphasizing the moral components of decisions will inspire executives to choose the moral path. But the common assumption this training is based on—that executives make explicit trade-offs between behaving ethically and earning profits for their organizations—is incomplete. This paradigm fails to acknowledge our innate psychological responses when faced with an ethical dilemma.

Findings from the emerging field of *behavioral ethics*—a field that seeks to understand how people actually behave when confronted with ethical dilemmas—offer insights that can round out our understanding of why we often behave contrary to our best ethical intentions. Our ethical behavior is often inconsistent, at times even hypocritical. Consider that people have the innate ability to maintain a belief while acting contrary to it.[5] Moral hypocrisy occurs when individuals' evaluations of their own moral transgressions differ substantially from their evaluations of the same transgressions committed by others. In one research study, participants were divided into two groups. In one condition, participants were required to distribute a resource (such as time or energy) to themselves and another person and could make the distribution fairly or unfairly. The "allocators" were then asked to evaluate the ethicality of their actions.

In the other condition, participants viewed another person acting in an unfair manner and subsequently evaluated the ethicality of this act. Individuals who made an unfair distribution perceived this transgression to be less objectionable than did those who saw another person commit the same transgression.[6] This widespread double standard—one rule for ourselves, a different one for others—is consistent with the gap that often exists between who we are and who we think that we should be.

Traditional approaches to ethics, and the traditional training methods that have accompanied such approaches, lack an understanding of the unintentional yet predictable cognitive patterns that result in unethical behavior. By contrast, our research on *bounded ethicality* focuses on the psychological processes that lead even good people to engage in ethically questionable behavior that contradicts their own preferred ethics. Bounded ethicality comes into play when individuals make decisions that harm others and when that harm is inconsistent with these decision makers' conscious beliefs and preferences. If ethics training is to actually change and improve ethical decision making, it needs to incorporate behavioral ethics, and specifically the subtle ways in which our ethics are bounded. Such an approach entails an understanding of the different ways our minds can approach ethical dilemmas and the different modes of decision making that result.

We have no strong opinion as to whether or not you, personally, are an ethical person. Rather, we aim to alert you to the blind spots that prevent all of us from seeing the gap between our own actual behavior and our desired behavior. In this book, we will provide substantial evidence that our ethical judgments are based on factors outside of our awareness. We will explore the implicit psychological processes that contribute to the gap between goals and behavior, as well as the role that organizations and political environments play in widening this divide. We will also offer tools to help weight important ethical decisions with greater reflection and less bias—at the individual level, the organizational level, and the societal level. We will then offer interventions that can more effectively improve the morality of decision making at each of these three levels.

What about You? The Implications of Ethical Gaps for Individuals

Most local and national journalists questioned in a recent survey expressed the strong belief that most reporters are more ethical than the politicians they cover. In stark contrast, most government and business leaders surveyed, including members of Congress, believed that reporters were no more ethical than the targets of their news stories.[7] Who's right? While it would be almost impossible to reach an objective conclusion, the vast literature that documents the way we view ourselves suggests that that both groups have inflated perceptions of their own ethicality.

Here's another question: Did former president George W. Bush act ethically or unethically when he decided to invade Iraq? How would you have answered this question during the early days of the war, when it looked as if the United States was "winning"? To what extent might political preferences bias answers to these questions? Most people believe they are fairly immune from bias when assessing the behavior of elected officials. Moreover, even when they try to recall their view at the time they made a decision, most people are affected by their knowledge of how well the decision turned out. Our preferences and biases affect how we assess ethical dilemmas, but we fail to realize that this is the case.

At this point, we may have convinced you that others have inflated perceptions of their own ethicality and a limited awareness of how their minds work. In all likelihood, though, you remain skeptical that this information applies to you. In fact, you probably are certain that you are as ethical as you have always believed yourself to be. To test this assumption, imagine that you have volunteered to participate in an experiment that requires you to try to solve a number of puzzles. You are told that you will be paid according to your performance, a set amount for each successfully solved puzzle. The experimenter mentions in passing that the research program is well funded. The experimenter also explains that, once you have finished the task, you will check your answers against an answer sheet, count the number of questions you answered correctly, put your answer sheet through a shredder, report the number of questions you solved correctly to the experimenter, and receive the money that you reported you earned.

Would you truthfully report the number of puzzles you solved to the experimenter, or would you report a higher number?[8] Note that there is no way for the experimenter to know if you cheated. While we do not know if you personally would cheat on this task, we do know that lots of seemingly nice people do cheat—just a little. In comparison to a group of individuals who are not allowed to shred their answers, those who are allowed to shred report that they solved significantly more problems than did those who didn't shred. Those who cheat likely count a problem they would have answered correctly, if only they hadn't made a careless mistake. Or they count a problem they would have aced if they only had had another ten seconds. And when piles of cash are present on a table in the room, participants are even more likely to cheat on the math task than when less money is visually available.[9] In this case, participants presumably justify their cheating on the grounds that the experimenters have money to burn. Ample evidence suggests that people who, in the abstract, believe they are honest and would never cheat, do in fact cheat when given such an easy, unverifiable opportunity to do so. These people aren't likely to factor this type of cheating into their assessments of their ethical character; instead, they leave the experiment with their positive self-image intact.

The notion that we experience gaps between who we believe ourselves to be and who we actually are is related to the problem of *bounded awareness*. Bounded awareness refers to the common tendency to exclude important and relevant information from our decisions by placing arbitrary and dysfunctional bounds around our definition of a problem.[10] Bounded awareness results in the systematic failure to see information that is relevant to our personal lives and professional obligations.

Figure 1. Photograph copyright © 1965 by Ronald C. James

Take a look at figure 1. What did you see? Now take a look at the Dalmatian sniffing on the ground. Most people do not see the Dalmatian on the first look. Once they know she is there, however, they easily see her—and, in fact, they can no longer look at the picture without noticing she is there. The context of the black-and-white background keeps us from noticing the Dalmatian, just as our profit-focused work environments can keep us from seeing the ethical implications of our actions.

As the Dalmatian picture demonstrates, we are "boundedly aware": our perceptions and decision making are constrained in ways we don't realize. In addition to falling prey to bounded awareness, recent research finds we are also subject to bounded ethicality, or systematic constraints on our morality that favor our own self-interest at the expense of the interest of others. As an example, a colleague of Ann's once mentioned that she had decided not to vaccinate her children given a perceived potential connection between vaccines and autism. After noting that this was a decision her colleague had a right to make, Ann suggested that she might be overweighing the risks of the vaccine in comparison to the risk of the disease. Ann also raised the possibility that her colleague was not fully considering the impact of her decision on others, particularly immune-compromised children who could die if they contracted diseases as commonplace as chicken pox from unvaccinated children. Several days later, Ann's colleague mentioned that she was rethinking her decision not to vaccinate her children, as she had never considered the other children who might be affected by her decision.

The psychological study of the mistakes of the mind helps to explain why a parent might overweigh the risks of a vaccine relative to the risk of a disease for the sake of her or his own child. Going a step further, bounded ethicality helps to explain how a parent might act in ways that violate her own ethical standards—by putting other people's children in danger—without being aware that she is doing so. We will explore how psychological tendencies produce this type of accidental unethical behavior.

Philosopher Peter Singer's book *The Life You Can Save: Acting Now to End World Poverty* provides ample documentation of how our limited awareness restricts our charitable giving and even our willingness to think about many ethical problems.[11] He opens his book with the following problem:

> On your way to work, you pass a small pond. On hot days, children sometimes play in the pond, which is only about knee-deep. The weather's cool today, though, and the hour is early, so you are surprised to see a child splashing about in the pond. As you get closer, you see that it is a very young child, just a toddler, who is flailing about, unable to stay upright or walk out of the pond. You look for the parents or babysitter, but there is no one else around. The child is unable to keep his head above the water for more than a few seconds at a time. If you don't wade in and pull him out, he seems likely to drown. Wading in is easy and safe, but you will ruin the new shoes you bought only a few days ago, and get your suit wet and muddy. By the time you hand the child over to someone responsible for him, and change your clothes, you'll be late for work. What should you do?

Singer notes that most people see this as an easy problem to solve. Clearly, one should jump in and save the child, as failing to do so would be a massive ethical failure. Singer then goes on to describe a challenge described by a man in Ghana:

> Take the death of this small boy this morning, for example. The boy died of measles. We all know he could have been cured at the hospital. But the parents had no money and so the boy died a slow and painful death, not of measles but out of poverty. Think about something like that happening 27,000 times every day. Some children die because they don't have enough to eat. More die, like that small boy in Ghana, from measles, malaria, diarrhea, and pneumonia, conditions that either don't exist in developed nations, or, if they do, are almost never fatal. The children are vulnerable to these diseases because they have no safe drinking water, or no sanitation, and because when they do fall ill, their parents can't afford any medical treatment. UNICEF, Oxfam, and many other organizations are working to reduce poverty and provide clean water and basic health care, and these efforts are reducing the toll. If the relief organizations had more money, they could do more, and more lives would be saved.

While one could quibble about whether the two stories are perfectly parallel, most people feel uncomfortable when reading this second story (we know that we were). In fact, the stories are quite similar, except for one difference. In the first, you would likely be aware of any gap that arises between what you should do and what you actually do: you should save the boy, and if you do not, it will be obvious to you that you failed to meet your own ethical standards. In the second example, your ethical blinders are firmly in place. Most people likely would be ashamed if they knew they had failed to save a life for a relatively small amount of money, yet most of us do exactly that. We will explore the psychological tendencies that produce those blind spots and suggest ways to remove them.

As another example, take the case of Bernard Madoff. Over the course of three decades, Madoff's Ponzi scheme racked up enormous losses:

more than 15,000 claims approaching $300 million in damages, and $64.8 billion in paper profit was wiped out. Madoff sold most of his investments through feeder funds—that is, other funds that either marketed their access to Madoff to potential investors or claimed they had access to some exotic investment strategy. In reality, the feeder funds were doing nothing more than turning much of the money they collected over to Madoff. These intermediaries were extremely well paid, often earning a small percentage of the funds invested plus 20 percent of any investment profits earned. Thus, as Madoff claimed an amazing record of success, the feeder funds were getting rich.

It is now clear that Madoff was a crook, and his purposeful, deceitful behavior lies outside of this book's focus on unintentional ethical behavior. Yet we are fascinated by the harmful behavior of so many other people in this story, people who had no intention of hurting Madoff's eventual victims. Many analysts have now concluded that outperforming all kinds of markets, as Madoff did, is statistically impossible. Did the managers of the feeder funds know that Madoff was running a Ponzi scheme, or did they simply fail to notice that Madoff's performance reached a level of return and stability that was impossible? Ample evidence suggests that many feeder funds had hints that something was wrong, but lacked the motivation to see the evidence that was readily available. For example, Rene-Thierry Magon de la Villehuchet, a descendent of European nobility and the CEO of Access International Advisors and Marketers, had invested his own money, his family's money, and money from his wealthy European clients with Madoff. He was repeatedly warned about Madoff and received ample evidence that Madoff's returns were not possible, but he turned a blind eye to the overwhelming evidence. Two weeks after Madoff surrendered to authorities, de la Villehuchet killed himself in his New York office.

Here's a final example of the type of psychological blind spots that affect us. In perhaps the most famous experiment in psychology, Stanley Milgram demonstrated the amazing degree to which people will engage in unethical behavior in order to fulfill their obligations to authority. Each participant in Milgram's study played the role of "teacher," while a study confederate (someone trained by the experimenter) played the role of "learner." The learner was portrayed as a forty-seven-year-old accountant. The teacher and learner were physically separated, such that the teacher could not see the learner. The teacher was told that it was his job to administer shocks of increasing magnitude, ranging from 15 volts to 450 volts, as the learner made mistakes in a task requiring the matching of word pairs.

The learner did make mistakes on the task, requiring the confederate to administer shocks. Up to 150 volts, occasional grunts were heard from the other side of the wall where the learner was located. (The learner was not actually receiving shocks; he was an actor.) At 150 volts, the learner shouted that he wanted to stop the experiment and let out some cries of pain. If the teacher resisted continuing, the experimenter insisted that the experiment must go on. From 150 to 300 volts, the teacher heard the learner as he pleaded to be released and complained about his heart condition. At 300 volts, the learner banged on the wall and demanded to be released. After 300 volts, the learner was completely silent.

Milgram surveyed psychiatrists, graduate students, behavioral science faculty members, college sophomores, and middle-class adults about their expectations of how study participants playing the role of the teacher would respond during the study. Across groups, survey respondents predicted that nearly all teachers would stop administering shocks well short of 450 volts. The psychiatrists predicted that nearly all teachers would refuse to move beyond the 150-volt level and that only one in a thousand participants would go all the way to 450 volts. In fact, in the actual study, 65 percent of those playing the role of teacher went all the way to 450 volts.[12] These powerful results show that our ethical behavior is distinctly different from our expectations of our own behavior. While many teachers were visibly upset and angry during the study, they nonetheless submitted to the experimenter's authority.

Milgram's study was replicated multiple times with more than 1,000 study participants. While the full experiment could not be replicated today, given much more stringent rules on the treatment of experimental subjects, a recent replication found that over 70 percent of contemporary study participants were willing to deliver at least 150 volts.[13] In addition, in 2010, producers of a French documentary invited people to participate in a television game show pilot called *Game of Death*. Unbeknown to the participants, the show was not real. Before it began, eighty participants signed contracts in which they agreed to inflict electric shocks on other contestants. With cameras rolling, and a crowd and the show's host egging them on, sixty-four of the eighty participants delivered severe enough shocks to a man (actually an actor) to the point that he appeared to be dead. Afterward, one of the participants admitted that she had followed orders even though her grandparents had been Jewish victims of the Holocaust.[14]

A recent analysis by Pat Werhane, Laura Hartman, Budhan Parmar, and Dennis Moberg reconsiders the Milgram experiments using a lens similar to the one we use in this book.[15] Rather than believing that study participants made an intentional decision to risk harming the learner in order to help the experimenter, this team argues that the teachers in the experiment had an incomplete mental model. Overly focused on following the instructions of the experimenter, many study participants failed to analyze the situation as an ethical dilemma.

In helping you to bring your own ethical gaps to light, we will expose you to the psychological processes that create your blind spots. More important, we identify effective strategies that take these psychological processes into account—including anticipating the influence of your impulses and learning how to accurately assess and learn from your past behavior. By removing common blinders, you can learn to do what you would think is right upon greater reflection.

What about Your Organization? The Implications of Ethical Gaps for Organizations

Because of the potential for widespread disaster, ethical gaps at the individual level are compounded when considered at the organizational level. One compelling example is the 1986 explosion of the *Challenger* space shuttle after it was launched at the lowest temperature in its history.[16] Extensive postcrash analyses documented that the explosion was caused because an O-ring on one of the shuttle's solid rocket boosters failed to seal at low temperatures.

On January 27, 1986, the night before the launch, engineers and managers from NASA and from shuttle contractor Morton Thiokol met to discuss whether it was safe to launch the *Challenger* at a low temperature. In seven of the shuttle program's twenty-four previous launches, problems with O-rings had been detected. Now, under intense time pressure, Morton Thiokol engineers hurriedly put together a presentation. They recommended to their superiors and to NASA personnel that the shuttle not be launched at low temperatures, citing their judgment that there was a connection between low temperature and the magnitude of these past O-ring problems.

NASA personnel reacted to the engineers' recommendation not to launch with hostility, according to Roger Boisjoly, a Morton Thiokol engineer who participated in the meeting.[17] In response to NASA's negative reaction to the recommendation not to launch, Morton Thiokol managers asked for the chance to caucus privately. "Just as [NASA manager] Larry Mulloy gave his conclusion," writes Boisjoly, Morton Thiokol manager "Joe Kilminster asked for a five-minute, off-line caucus to re-evaluate the data and as soon as the mute button was pushed, our general manager, Jerry Mason, said in a soft voice, 'We have to make a management decision.'"

In the caucus that followed, "No one in management wanted to discuss the facts," writes an incensed Boisjoly.[18] In his opinion, his superiors were primarily focused on pleasing their customer, NASA, which had placed Morton Thiokol in the position of proving that it was not safe to fly rather than the more typical default of not launching until there was reason to believe it was safe to fly.[19] "The managers were struggling to make a list of data that would support a launch decision," Boisjoly writes, "but unfortunately for them, the data actually supported a no-launch decision."[20] Against the objections of their own engineers, the four Morton

Thiokol senior managers present voted to recommend the launch. They gave their recommendation to NASA, which quickly accepted the recommendation to launch.

Perhaps the most startling aspect of this story is the data that engineers analyzed when trying to determine whether low temperatures were connected to O-ring failure. NASA and Morton Thiokol engineers argued about the possible role of temperature based on the fact that low temperatures were present during many of the seven launches that had O-ring problems. Many of the engineers on both teams saw no clear observable pattern regarding the O-rings. These were well-experienced engineers with rigorous analytic training. They were talented enough to know that, to find out whether outdoor temperature was related to engine failure, they should examine temperatures when problems occurred and temperatures when they did not. Yet no one at NASA or Morton Thiokol asked for the temperatures for the seventeen past launches in which an O-ring failure had *not* occurred. An examination of *all* of the data shows a clear connection between temperature and O-ring failure, and that the *Challenger* had a 99 percent chance of failure. But because the engineers were constrained in their thinking, they only looked at a subset of the available data and missed the connection.

The failure of NASA and Morton Thiokol engineers to look outside the bounds of the data in the room was an error committed by well-intentioned people that caused seven astronauts to lose their lives and delivered an enormous blow to the space program. It is common for decision makers to err by limiting their analysis to the data in the room, rather than asking what data would best answer the question being asked. These decision makers were guilty of a common form of bounded ethicality: moving forward too quickly with readily available information, rather than first asking what data would be relevant to answer the question on the table and how the decision would affect other aspects of the situation or other people.

An organization's ethical gap is more than just the sum of the individual ethical gaps of its employees. Group work, the building block of organizations, creates additional ethical gaps. Groupthink—the tendency for cohesive groups to avoid a realistic appraisal of alternative courses of action in favor of unanimity—can prevent groups from challenging questionable decisions, as was the case with NASA's decision to launch the *Challenger*.[21]

In addition, functional boundaries prevent individuals from viewing a problem as an ethical one. Organizations often segment decisions within particular groups or disperse different aspects of a decision to different parts of the organization. As a result, the typical ethical dilemma tends to be viewed as an engineering, marketing, or financial problem, even when the ethical relevance is obvious to other groups. Morton Thiokol general manager Jerry Mason reportedly decided to treat the question of whether to launch the *Challenger* as a "management decision." This perspective enabled him and others at the final prelaunch meeting to fade the ethical dimensions of the problem from consideration, as if it were possible to ignore the human lives at stake. Such fading prevents employees who make seemingly innocuous decisions from recognizing the ethical implications of their decisions for others. Only when the boundaries are removed does the ethical import of the decision become clear. Armed with an understanding of the reasons ethical fading occurs, employees can uncover the powerful and often dangerous informal values that influence their behavior and effectively diagnose the ethical "sinkholes" in their organizations.

What about Society? The Implications of Ethical Gaps for Society

Policy decisions may be the most important set of decisions we make as a society. Yet, in this realm, blind spots can play an active, dysfunctional role without our conscious awareness.[22] For example, consider the case of organ donation, adapted from a problem that Max wrote with his colleagues:[23]

Which option do you prefer?

A. If you die in an accident, your heart and other organs will be used to save other lives. In addition, if you ever need an organ transplant, there will be a 90 percent chance that you will get the organ.

B. If you die in an accident, you will be buried with your heart and other organs in your body. In addition, if you ever need an organ transplant, there will be a 45 percent chance that you will get the organ.

Most of us have a reflexive preference for option A. That's a good thing, as a change in the U.S. organ donation system to one resembling option A could save up to 6,000 lives per year in the United States alone—roughly twice as many people as were killed in the 9/11 attacks. Nonetheless, the United States continues to follow an organ donation policy that looks more like option B. Why? In the United States, if you die in an accident and have made no explicit decision about your organs, you will be buried (or cremated) with your organs intact. If you want to donate your organs, you need to proactively *opt in* to the donation system (typically, when you renew your driver's license). In contrast, in many European nations, if you make no explicit decision about organ donation, your organs are available for harvesting. In these countries, you need to proactively *opt out* of the system if you want to keep your organs after death. In both cases, you have a choice, assuming you stop to think about it and fill out the right form accordingly, but the default option differs. The opt-in system roughly creates option B, while the opt-out system roughly creates option A.

As figure 2 shows, the default option leads to large and appalling differences in donation rates across counties. What about the United States? Our organ donation consent rate is 44 percent—pretty good for an opt-in nation, but dreadful in comparison to what could so easily be obtained through a simple change in mind-set. (In case you are wondering why Sweden's donation consent rate is lower than that of other opt-out na-

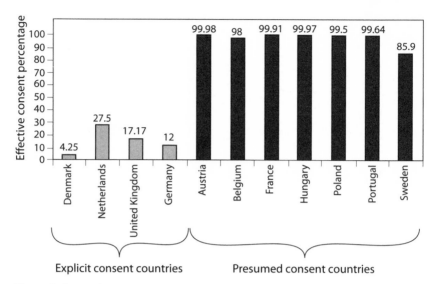

Figure 2. Organ donation across European countries. From E. J. Johnson and D. Goldstein (2003), "Do Defaults Save Lives?" *Science* 302:1338–39. Reprinted with permission from AAAS.

tions, it is because Sweden gives the survivors of the deceased a greater opportunity to decline to donate.)

The number of lives that potentially could be saved in the United States—6,000 annually—from a simple change in the laws is a poignant example of the role that society can play in creating and perpetuating blind spots. While there may be insightful, honest people who are opposed to organ donation for religious or moral reasons, our focus is on the plethora of citizens and leaders who would prefer option A upon reflection, yet who stand by while our nation continues to resort to option B.

As concerned members of society, all of us want the individuals and organizations that represent us to behave ethically. Yet those making decisions that affect society tend to be unaware of the blind spots that prevent them from doing just that. Consider a story involving Supreme Court justice Antonin Scalia. In March 2004, the Sierra Club filed a motion asking Scalia to recuse himself from the *Cheney v. U.S. District Court* case on the grounds that Scalia had hunted ducks in Louisiana with Vice President Dick Cheney in January 2004. The Supreme Court had agreed to hear the case of whether Cheney should be forced to provide information about the energy task force he led while the Bush administration was formulating its environmental policy. The Sierra Club made the obvious case that Scalia and Cheney's friendship could affect Scalia's objectivity. But Scalia refused to recuse himself; he insisted that his friendship with the vice president would not distort his judgment and did not violate the Supreme Court's rules on conflict of interest. "If it is reasonable to think that a Supreme Court justice can be bought so cheap," Scalia commented, "the nation is in deeper trouble than I had imagined."[24]

Scalia's comments indicate that he rejects or is unaware of the unambiguous evidence on the psychological aspects of conflicts of interest. Even more troubling than this lack of understanding are the Supreme Court's rules, which, like most guidelines and laws that are intended to protect against conflicts of interest, guard only against *intentional* corruption.[25] Yet most instances of corruption, and unethical behavior in general, are unintentional, a product of bounded ethicality and the fading of the ethical dimension of the problem. For this reason, the laws on intentional corruption are of relatively little use in protecting society.

Bounded Ethicality: Implications at Three Levels of Analysis

The implications of failing to consider our ethical gaps is compounded when we consider all three levels—individual, organizational, and societal—simultaneously. Consider the following story:

Imagine that you are fifty-five years old and you've just been diagnosed with early-stage cancer. You investigate all of the treatment options available to you, consulting three prominent doctors in different fields, and quickly realize that you are facing the most important decision of your life. The surgeon suggests that you operate to try to remove the cancer. The radiologist thinks you should blast the cancer with radiation. The homeopathic doctor believes you should use less intrusive medicine and wait to see how the cancer develops. How could three renowned doctors recommend such different treatments?

In his memoir, *Swimming Across*, Andy Grove, the former chairperson of Intel, described facing this very problem when he was diagnosed with prostate cancer in 1995. Grove had the resources, financial and otherwise, to find the best cure possible. He set about meeting with top physicians representing each of the three possible courses of treatment recommended to him. Each physician strongly recommended that Grove undertake the type of intervention that he or she would personally perform.[26]

At the heart of this situation is an ethical dilemma. Consider that each doctor is likely to view the problem in terms of advising the patient on the best possible treatment available, without seeing the problem as one with ethical import. At the same time, each doctor is biased toward advocating a treatment plan based on his or her own area of expertise. The dilemma isn't that doctors are lying to patients in order to drum up business. Clearly, doctors have strong convictions about their recommendations. They treat the same illness, yet each believes his or her preferred treatment is superior, and they fail to recognize that their beliefs are biased in a self-serving manner. In other words, they don't recognize that they're facing an ethical dilemma: whether to recommend *their* treatment or the *best* treatment for this patient. They fail to realize that their training, incentives, and preferences prevent them from offering objective advice.

Conflicts of interest have captured the attention of the medical community, and in Washington, Senator Charles Grassley (R-Iowa) has condemned medical schools and other organizations for not doing more to address the issue. Under our current system, doctors have financial incentives to prescribe drugs and treatments that are not in the best interest of the patient. Yet most smart, well-educated doctors are puzzled by the criticism against them, as they are confident in their own ethicality and the "fact" that they always put their patients' interests first. Doctors, like professionals in other fields, such as Justice Scalia, tend to view conflicts

of interest as a problem of intentional corruption. But the more perni-
cious aspect of conflicts of interest is clarified by well-replicated research
showing that when people have a vested interest in seeing a problem in a
certain manner, they are no longer capable of objectivity. Most doctors,
like most people, are affected by conflicts of interest, make biased treatment decisions, and do so without any awareness of the ethical dimensions of their decisions. They honestly believe they are putting their patients' interests first.

Why do we, as a society, continue to tolerate conflicts of interest in so
many life-and-death realms? Most people like to find a single explanation
for a given social problem, whether it's poverty or homelessness or teenage pregnancy. University of Chicago professor Ann McGill illustrates
this cognitive bias with the extreme example of people arguing endlessly
over whether teenage promiscuity or lack of birth control causes teenage
pregnancy, when the obvious answer is that both cause the problem.[27]
Similarly, there is no single explanation for ethical dilemmas; rather,
blind spots form at several levels of analysis: individual, organizational,
and societal.

At the individual level, as we have already suggested, we fall prey to
psychological processes that bias our decisions—and, more importantly,
we don't know they are biased.

At the organizational level, business leaders typically fail to appreciate
the role of bounded ethicality in their employees' decisions. Furthermore,
they typically believe that their employees' integrity will protect them and
the organization from ethical infractions. Yet many ethical infractions are
rooted in the intricacies of human psychology rather than integrity. To
design wise interventions, leaders need to consider the ways in which
their current environment could prompt unethical action without the decision maker's conscious awareness.

At the societal level, when individuals and their organizations cannot
or will not solve these problems, doing so becomes the job of the federal
government. When the government fails to grapple with the bounded
ethicality of individuals, organizations, and industries, effective solutions

will remain out of reach. Across industries, the psychological processes that lead to ethical fading and bounded ethicality must be considered. Doing so requires making changes to societal defaults that highlight the value trade-offs we are making and draw attention to future concerns.

What's to Come

In this chapter, we have deliberately avoided offering a definition of the term "ethics" or distinguishing between ethics and morality. You can find such definitions and distinctions elsewhere. We don't claim to hold the key to what constitutes moral truth, and we have no interest in changing your ethics to match our own.[28] Rather than presenting our own ideas of what constitutes ethical or moral behavior, we are interested in highlighting the broad array of reasons that people behave in ways that may be inconsistent with their *own* personal values.

We also have no interest in constraining the advice of physicians or any other group of experts. It would be overly simplistic to remind trained professionals that their decisions should be based on the best interest of their patients, clients, and constituents rather than on financial incentives. Rather, our motive is to convince individuals—including physicians, CEOs, accountants, consultants, politicians, and all citizens—that they are affected by blind spots that prevent them from meeting their own ethical standards. Most of us behave ethically most of the time. At other times, we are aware when we behave unethically. This book focuses on more dangerous situations: the times when we unwittingly behave unethically. Chapter 2 will connect our perspective to existing theories of ethical thought. In chapter 3, we will caution you about bounded ethicality and the internal limits the human mind places on ethical behavior. In chapter 4, we will expose the mental tricks that lead to ethical fading. In chapter 5, we will present evidence that our ethical blinders not only prevent us from seeing our own ethical gaps, but also the ethical gaps of those around us. In chapter 6 and 7, we will discuss how organizations and governments exacerbate unethical behavior. We will conclude, in chapter 8, by offering advice at the individual, organizational, and societal levels on how to eliminate your blind spots and view the ethical dilemmas in your life more clearly.

Chapter 2

Why Traditional Approaches to Ethics Won't Save You

Imagine that you are standing on a footbridge spanning some trolley tracks (see figure 3). You see that a runaway trolley is threatening to kill five people. Standing next to you, in between the oncoming trolley and the five people, is a railway worker wearing a large backpack. You quickly realize that the only way to save the people is to push this man off the bridge and onto the tracks below. The man will die, but his body will stop the trolley from reaching the others. (You quickly understand that you can't jump yourself because you aren't carrying enough weight to stop the trolley, and there's no time to put on the man's backpack.) Legal concerns aside, would it be ethical for you to save the five people by pushing this stranger to his death?

We have just described a very famous philosophy problem known as the "footbridge dilemma."[1] It is often used to contrast two different nor-

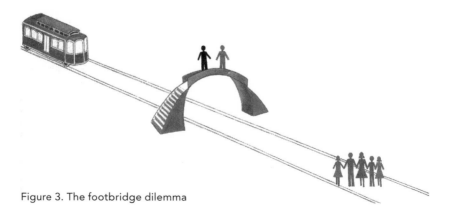

Figure 3. The footbridge dilemma

mative approaches to ethical decision making: a *consequentalist* approach and a *deontological* approach. A *consequentalist* approach is one that determines the morality of an action by its ensuing consequences. Utilitarianism, a common form of consequentalialism, is often described by the phrase "doing the greatest good for the greatest number of people." A very different form of ethical thinking, what Immanuel Kant referred to as *deontological* approach, judges the morality of an action based on the action's adherence to rules or duties.[2] Kant argued that judgments of whether an act is right or wrong should be determined by a consideration of rights and duties in society. From Kant's point of view, the act of pushing someone off of a bridge would violate his rights and is therefore immoral.

Indeed, when reading the footbridge dilemma, most people do not believe it is ethically acceptable to push the railway worker off the bridge in order to save five lives. Using a deontological approach, they ask themselves whether they have the right to push someone off of a bridge. If you ask them why they are opposed to the idea of pushing the man off the bridge, common answers include, "That would be murder!" "The ends don't justify the means!" or "People have rights!"[3] By contrast, a utilitarian approach would involve adding up the costs and benefits of each choice and choosing the option that yields the best balance of costs and benefits for all involved—which, in this case, would be to save five lives at the expense of one.

Now let's look at a problem that was conceived before the footbridge dilemma, the "trolley dilemma": A runaway trolley is headed for five railway workmen who will be killed if it proceeds on its present course (see figure 4). The only way to save these people is to hit a switch that will turn the trolley onto a side track where it will run over and kill one workman instead of five. Ignoring legal concerns, would it be ethically acceptable for you to turn the trolley by hitting the switch in order to save five people at the expense of one person?[4]

When considering the trolley dilemma, most people (who have not previously been exposed to the footbridge dilemma) say that it is ethically permissible to hit the switch. If you ask them why, their explanations tend

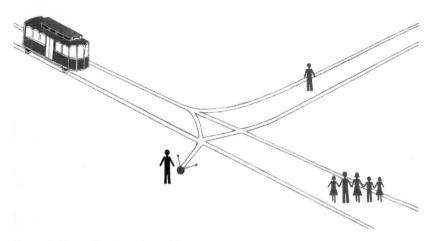

Figure 4. The trolley (switch) problem

to focus on the belief that having five people die would be worse than having one person die.[5] This is prototypical *utilitarian* thinking because of its focus on the consequences of actions.

When people are exposed to both of these problems, some are bothered by the arguable inconsistency of deciding to flip the switch to turn the trolley (in the trolley dilemma), contrasted with the decision not to push the man over the bridge (in the footbridge dilemma). Those who are bothered by the inconsistency tend to make the footbridge decision intuitively; later exposure to the trolley dilemma then leads them to greater reflection consistent with utilitarian reasoning. As these two stories illustrate, we sometimes use the implied philosophical principles discussed earlier to make judgments. However, we tend to apply these rules inconsistently, and we sometimes violate what we would do if we gave the question more thought.

We have no vested stake in whether you are more of a utilitarian or a deontologist, or if you decide to become one or the other upon finishing this book. You are welcome to your own opinion about what to do in the footbridge and trolley problems. Our aim is simply to alert readers to potential inconsistencies in their decisions and actions—and, in particular, to the gap that exists between their behavior and their perceptions of their behavior, a gap that traditional ethical approaches tend to ignore.

Can Ethicists Improve Our Ethics?

After the collapse of Enron and other organizations during the same period, professional schools and corporations have been called on to give ethical matters more serious deliberation. As society demands more ethical behavior from organizations, it is useful to examine whether traditional ethical analysis offers a promising solution. The first logical step in this process is to examine what ethicists have to offer to the issue. Within the field of philosophy, ethics has historically been studied from a normative perspective—that is, an approach that seeks to determine the morally correct course of action. This type of perspective focuses on asking the question, "How should people behave?" Philosophers have considered, for example, whether a utilitarian or deontological approach to the footbridge dilemma is more appropriate.

Contemporary philosophers have argued that philosophical thinking is central to a moral education, that it will make us better citizens, and that it will give us the courage needed to stand up for justice.[6] Yet legal scholar and judge Richard Posner argues that no empirical evidence exists to support these claims.[7] In fact, ethicists themselves provide the perfect sample to test whether traditional, normative training in ethics leads to more ethical behavior, notes Eric Schwitzgebel, a philosophy professor at the University of California at Riverside. Because ethicists devote their careers to studying and teaching morality, we might expect ethicists to behave more ethically than the rest of us.[8]

Yet in his research, Schwitzgebel finds that if morality is equated with "not stealing," ethicists do not score very well, at least by certain measures. Surveying thirty-one leading academic libraries in the United States and the United Kingdom, Schwitzgebel compared the rate at which ethics books were missing from the shelves to the rate at which nonethics books in philosophy, comparable in age and popularity, were missing. He found that ethics books were more likely to be missing than nonethics books. Next, he examined the presence of fairly obscure philosophical texts that would likely be borrowed only by advanced students and professors. Among those texts, he found that a philosophy book was 50 to 150 percent more likely to be missing if it was an ethics book than if it was a nonethics book.

Schwitzgebel conducted related research on whether ethicists are more likely to engage in the arguably prosocial behaviors of voting and not eating meat. Comparing philosophical ethicists with both other philosophers and with professors in other departments, he found that while ethicists were more likely to condemn meat-eating than were other nonethicist philosophers and other academics, they were no less likely to eat meat themselves. Across other contexts, the researcher found little support for the notion that traditional ethics training creates more ethical citizens.[9] Schwitzgebel concluded that his research undercuts the widespread assumption that enrollment in ethics courses will improve students' future ethical behavior.[10]

Even professional philosophers appear to be divided regarding the ethical behavior of ethicists. A poll of philosophers at an American Philosophical Association meeting in April 2007 found that although a substantial minority (especially ethicists) expressed the view that ethicists do behave morally better, on average, than nonethicists of a similar social background, a majority of respondents said that ethicists do *not* behave better than nonethicists.[11]

Surprised? You might not be if you thought about the focus and underlying assumptions of a philosophical approach to ethics. Normative ethicists from a philosophical tradition have focused on exploring how we *should* behave and have made great strides toward answering these types of questions. However, little empirical attention has been devoted to examining how people actually *do* behave and how their ethical behavior can be improved—knowledge that is needed to understand and improve not just how philosophers behave, but also how the ethical and economic crises of the past decade emerged. As we will discuss later in this book, how we think we *should* behave is very different from how we *want* to behave. We may predict we will behave in a manner consistent with our expectations for ourselves. But when the time comes to make a decision, we often behave the way we want to behave.

The Limits of Traditional Approaches to Ethics

Another barrier that has kept scholars of ethics from fully dealing with ethical issues concerns the central role they give to decision makers' ethical intentions. Most approaches to ethics assume that people recognize an ethical dilemma for what it is and respond to it intentionally. By contrast, research on *bounded ethicality* examines unethical behavior that arises without intentionality. Consider J. R. Rest's influential descriptive model of ethical decision making. Rest claims that individuals faced with ethical decisions go through the following four phases:[12]

Moral Awareness → Moral Judgment → Moral Intention → Moral Action

Moral awareness, judgment, intention, and action certainly are important factors in understanding many ethical decisions. Yet this model is incomplete and potentially misleading. The model presumes that (1) awareness is needed for a decision to have moral implications, (2) an individual's reasoning determines judgment, and (3) moral intention is required for her to understand her moral action. Each of these assumptions, which are implicit in traditional approaches to ethics and many ethical training programs, ignores evidence to the contrary. In doing so, the model directs our attention away from critical elements of decision making and judgment that lead to unethical behavior. As we explain in the sections that follow, those who teach us to behave more ethically neglect many of the situations in which we actually find ourselves, including those where we lack moral awareness, judge before reasoning, and misjudge moral intention.

When We Lack Moral Awareness

Imagine that you are a salesperson who works on full commission. All of your income depends on how much you sell. You have been given aggressive sales quotas, and you focus on how to meet these goals. At the end of the year, you accomplish these goals and are rewarded generously by your company.

This scenario describes the situation faced by millions of employees working for organizations around the world. At face value, the situation appears completely acceptable. Now let's add more detail. The year is 2006, the salesperson is a mortgage lender, and his quotas require him to lend money to homeowners independent of their ability to pay. Or imagine that the salesperson works at Enron in 1999, selling a new concept: the firm's "special purpose entities," or shell firms—ways to hide its debt—to private equity investors such as JPMorgan Chase, Citigroup, Credit Suisse First Boston, and Wachovia.

While some of the salespeople at these companies were probably aware of the ethical consequences of their decisions, many more were probably unaware. They may have viewed them as "business decisions" and believed they were following accepted practices to achieve the ultimate business goal of making money. Or they may have seen them as legal decisions and asked themselves merely whether the sales strategies they followed were technically legal. It's likely that most didn't, however, view these decisions as ethical ones.

Training in business ethics tends to be largely based on the approaches to ethics described above: that is, emphasizing the moral components of decisions with the goal of encouraging executives to choose the moral path. But the common assumption that this training is based on—that executives make explicit trade-offs between behaving ethically and earning profits for their organizations—is too narrow. It ignores the fact that decision makers often fail to see the "ethics" in a given ethical dilemma. In many situations, decision makers do not recognize the need to apply the type of ethical judgment they may have learned in ethics training courses to their decision-making process.

As we described in chapter 1, our minds are subject to *bounded ethical-ity,* or cognitive limitations that can make us unaware of the moral implications of our decisions. The outside world also limits our ability to see the ethical dimensions of particular decisions. For example, aspects of everyday work life—including goals, rewards, compliance systems, and informal pressures—can contribute to *ethical fading,* a process by which ethical dimensions are eliminated from a decision.[13] Ann and her colleague Dave Messick have argued that these common features of organizations can blind us to the ethical implications of a decision, leading us, for example, to classify a decision as a "business decision" rather than an "ethical decision" and thus increasing the likelihood that we will behave unethically.

The organizational practices that contribute to ethical fading may be as subtle as differences in the language used to describe the decision. A case in point is Albert Speer, one of Adolf Hitler's government ministers and most trusted advisers. After the war, Speer admitted that by labeling himself an "administrator" of Hitler's plan, he convinced himself that issues relating to human beings were not part of his job.[14] This labeling allowed Speer to reclassify ethical decisions as business decisions, such that the ethical dimensions faded from the decision.

Why does our classification of a decision matter? Because classification often affects the decisions that follow. When we fail to recognize a decision as an ethical one, whether due to our own cognitive limitations or because external forces cause ethical fading, this failure may very well affect how we analyze the decision and steer us toward unintended, unethical behavior.

When We Judge before Reasoning

Consider the following two stories:

- A woman is cleaning out her closet, and she finds her old U.S. flag. She doesn't want the flag anymore, so she cuts it up into pieces and uses the rags to clean her bathroom.
- A family's dog is killed by a car in front of their house. They have heard that dog meat is delicious, so they cut up the dog's body and cook it and eat it for dinner.

When psychologist Jonathan Haidt and his colleagues presented these stories to study participants, most of them immediately decried the behaviors depicted to be wrong, though they couldn't immediately offer informative explanations for their opinions.[15] Instead, they responded with statements such as, "I don't know, I can't explain it, I just know."[16]

Intuitionist psychologists such as Haidt argue that such emotional reactions precede moral judgment. In other words, moral reasoning doesn't influence moral judgment. Rather, it's the other way around: moral judgment influences moral reasoning. According to this view, quick, emotional reactions drive our judgments, and it is only after making such judgments that we engage in deliberate moral reasoning to justify our initial reaction.[17] These emotive processes generate our initial verdicts about ethical issues, such as the use of the flag and consumption of dogs. In direct contradiction of the Rest model of ethical decision making, only after reaching these verdicts do we come up with reasons to explain them.

The strong influence of emotional reactions on moral judgment is supported by research showing that individuals with neurological damage to the regions of the brain responsible for emotion have a reduced capacity for moral judgment and behavior.[18] These findings cast doubt on the notion that judgment always precedes action, a premise that has dominated traditional approaches to ethics.

When We Misjudge Moral Intention

Traditional philosophical approaches to ethics, particularly certain segments of deontological ethics, place intention as a central consideration in judgments of unethical behavior. That is, when judging an individual's ethicality, these approaches consider whether or not the person intended to behave ethically. But consider that judgments of intentions can be based on erroneous factors, as this example developed by Yale University philosophy professor Joshua Knobe illustrates:[19]

> The chairman of a company has to decide whether to adopt a new program. It would increase profits and help the environment too. "I don't care at all about helping the environment," the chairman says.

"I just want to make as much profit as I can. Let's start the new program." Would you say that the chairman intended to help the environment?

Now consider a variation on the situation.

The chairman has decided to adopt a new program. The program would increase profits but harm the environment. "I don't care at all about helping the environment," the chairman says. "I just want to make as much profit as I can. Let's start the new program." Would you say that the chairman intended to harm the environment?

Despite the fact that, in both scenarios, the chairman's only goal is to make money, people's judgments of the chairman's intention seem to depend on the "side effect" of the chairman's decision. After study respondents read the first scenario, in which the program led to environmental improvements, only 23 percent said the chairman had intentionally helped the environment. By contrast, after respondents read the second scenario, 82 percent believed the chairman had intentionally harmed the environment. This was true despite the fact that the chairman expressed identical intentions in both scenarios.

Such inconsistencies are driven by factors irrelevant to a decision maker's intentions. As such, they cast doubt on approaches that make intentionality a defining characteristic of ethical versus unethical behavior. It's true that intentionality can drive responses to ethical behavior, but that is not true for all situations and all decisions. As Ann and her colleague Kristin Smith-Crowe have argued, "'good' and 'bad' people make 'good' and 'bad' decisions." Therefore it's important to be able to identify and understand intentional *and* unintentional ethical decisions. Traditional approaches neglect the latter.

The variables that the Rest model of ethical decision making encapsulates are important. But some of the model's elements—moral awareness, a set order of stages, and intentionality—obscure key factors that lead to unethical behaviors in organizational life. By ignoring ethical decisions that occur without moral awareness, the model leaves a substantial portion of unethical decisions, and the reasons behind them, unexamined.

A subset of a new school of philosophy that examines actual behavior, known as *experimental philosophy*, responds to some of our criticisms. These philosophical rebels, in hopes of shedding light on traditional philosophical issues, run experiments to gather information about the judgments that people actually make when faced with moral dilemmas.[20] This type of research should provide valuable information on how people actually behave. At this stage, however, it represents a small and somewhat isolated subset of philosophers whose work has yet to affect traditional approaches to ethics training.

If philosophical approaches don't provide all of the keys needed to reduce unethical behavior in organizations, what will? Unlocking the door to unethical behavior requires an insightful understanding of the subtle influences on our behavior—influences of which we are often unaware—and their impact on how we think about ethical dilemmas. In the next section and chapters that follow, we describe how psychologists are applying those insights to the burgeoning field of behavioral ethics.

Two Cognitive Systems, Two Modes of Decision Making

The field of behavioral ethics emphasizes the need to consider how individuals actually make decisions rather than how they would make decisions in an ideal world. Research reveals that our minds have two distinct modes of decision making. By understanding these modes, we can reach key insights to help improve the ethicality of our decisions.

Not surprisingly, decision making tends to be most ethically compromised when our minds are overloaded. The busier you are at work, for example, the less likely you will be to notice when a colleague cuts ethical corners or when you yourself go over the line. An important psychological concept sheds light on why this tends to be the case: the distinction between "System 1" and "System 2" thinking.[21] According to this view, System 1 thinking is our intuitive system of processing information: fast, automatic, effortless, implicit, and emotional. System 1 is also efficient, and thus serves as an appropriate tool for the vast majority of decisions we make on a daily basis. By comparison, System 2 thinking is slower, conscious, effortful, explicit, and more logical.[22] When you weigh the costs and benefits of alternative courses of action in a systematic and organized manner, you are engaging in System 2 thinking.

It is quite common for people to have emotional, System 1 responses to ethical problems. However, such responses are sometimes at odds with what we would have decided with more deliberation. Moreover, the importance of real-world decisions does not necessarily protect us from the limits of the human mind. In fact, the frantic pace of modern life can lead us to rely on System 1 thinking even when System 2 thinking is warranted.[23] In one study, researchers found that "cognitively busy" study participants were more likely to cheat on a task than were less overloaded study participants.[24] Why? Because it takes cognitive energy to be reflective enough to stop one's impulse to cheat. Kern and Chugh found that the impact of outside influences on our ethical choices—such as whether the same outcome is framed as a loss or a gain—depends on how much time we have to make the decision.[25] They asked people to imagine themselves in the following situation:

> You are trying to sell your stereo to raise money for an upcoming trip overseas. The stereo works great, and an audiophile friend tells you that if he were in the market for stereo equipment (which he isn't), he'd give you $500 for it. You don't have a lot of time before you leave for your trip. Your friend advises that you have a 25% chance of getting the sale before you leave for your trip. [A separate group was told that they would have a 75% chance of losing the sale.] A few days later, the first potential buyer comes to see the stereo and seems interested. The potential buyer asks if you have any other offers. How likely are you to respond by saying that you do have another offer?

As in other research by Kern and Chugh, study participants were more willing to cheat to avoid losses ("losing the sale") than to accrue gains ("getting the sale"). However, the framing as a loss or a gain only affected decision making when individuals were under time pressure and told to respond as quickly as they could. Individuals who were under no such pressure—those who were told to take their time in responding and to think carefully about the question—were not affected by the irrelevant framing (irrelevant to the choice as an ethical one) of a potential gain versus a potential loss.

Which way of thinking is better, System 1 or System 2? Many people were pleased when author Malcolm Gladwell made a case for trusting our intuition in his book *Blink*. We like to go with our gut (System 1). Moreover, System 1 thinking is sufficient for most decisions; it would be a waste of time to logically think through every choice we make while shopping for groceries, for instance. However, trusting our gut instinctively, without ever employing System 2 thinking, can widen the gap between how we want to behave and how we actually behave. System 2 logic should be part of our most important decisions, including those with ethical import.

If your gut reaction is different from the decision you reach after more deliberative processing, it is important to reconcile this inconsistency. If you let your gut rule, something as simple as whether a choice is framed as a gain or a loss might influence a decision. But if you ignore your gut and completely base your decision only on a cold calculation of the costs and benefits, you may be ignoring internal warning signs that "something isn't right," such as the omission of the decision's ethical implications from the calculation—the type of signs to which those who contributed to the financial crisis of 2008 should have listened. It's important to get the two systems to talk to each other. Essentially, when the two systems disagree, that is your hint to have each system "audit" the other system. Your gut can help you figure out what feelings you may have left out of your careful calculation, and rational analysis may help you determine whether irrelevant factors are influencing your gut response.

The Importance of Ethical Self-Awareness

As evidenced by the research findings presented in this chapter, people generally fail to recognize that their ethical judgments are biased in ways they would condemn with greater awareness. Unfortunately, informing us about our biases doesn't seem to help us make better choices. We tend to believe that while others may fall prey to such inconsistencies, we ourselves are immune to them. For example, when participants in one study were asked to predict whether financial incentives would influence their own and others' decisions to donate blood, most overestimated the influence of self-interest on others; at the same time, they denied it would affect their own decision.[26] Most of us dramatically underestimate the degree to which our behavior is affected by incentives and other situational factors.

The decisions we make on behalf of ourselves, our organizations, and society at large can create great harm. To improve our ethical judgment, we need to understand and accept the limitations of the human mind. Yet the solutions that have been offered to reduce the undesirable outcomes of these decisions—including laws and ethics remediation and training—don't take these limitations into account. Without an awareness of blind spots, traditional approaches to ethics won't be particularly useful in improving behavior. If, like most people, you routinely fail to recognize the ethical components of decisions, succumb to common cognitive biases, and think you behave more unethically that you actually do, then being taught which ethical judgment you should make is unlikely to improve your ethicality. By contrast, the lessons of behavioral ethics should prove useful for those who wish to be more ethical human beings but whose judgments don't always live up to their ideals or expectations.

Chapter 3

When We Act against Our Own Ethical Values

As professors, we often receive telephone calls from long-lost friends or relatives as one of their children's eighteenth birthday approaches. Why do these calls so often arrive around this particular time frame? Well, it turns out that these calls disproportionately come from friends and relatives whose children just happen to be applying to our universities. Of course, our friends explain that they know we don't have the power to admit their child; they are only calling to request a letter of recommendation or an introduction to the director of admissions.

These calls are awkward for us. Because we typically do not know the applicant well, it is unlikely that our input would be of much use to the admissions office. At the same time, it would be unpleasant to tell a second cousin that, despite what our relatives may have said about our importance at the university, we can offer little help. So since we have met the dean of admissions before, we follow through with the awkward process of making arrangements to introduce the applicant to the dean.

How would you rate us on "niceness" for making such introductions? What about our ethical behavior?

Perhaps you have been asked to do favors for friends, or friends of friends, or friends of relatives. Perhaps those favors involved the allocation of scarce resources (such as jobs), admission to select groups (such as universities), an apartment in a desirable location, or an introduction to a loan officer at a bank. Most of us have received such requests at one time or another. Research shows that we are intuitively most comfortable doing favors for those with whom we identify—that is, with people who are a lot like us. Psychologists refer to this phenomenon as *in-group favoritism*. In particular, we tend to be biased toward people who share our alma mater, religion, race, or gender.

Turning our attention to race, consider that minorities tend to be underrepresented at the top levels of companies and on the faculties of most universities. This suggests that, in these settings, Caucasians are most commonly making phone calls to Caucasians to request special favors for Caucasians, leaving minorities out in the cold. When our friends and relatives call us asking for special favors for their children, we have no intention of excluding underrepresented minorities. In fact, we probably don't think at all about the minorities who will be affected by our actions; rather, we focus on how "nice" we are being by putting in a good word to the dean of admissions on behalf of our long-lost third cousin once removed. But when resources are scarce, and we favor people who are similar to us, the net result is discrimination against those who are different from us. In essence, favoring those who resemble us demographically is equivalent to punishing those who do not share our demographic traits. Yet most of us fail to recognize this fact.

Consider that over the last two decades, a common finding in the mortgage lending business has been that banks are much more likely to deny a mortgage to an African American than to a Caucasian, even after controlling for income, house location, and so on. When this effect was first reported in the 1990s, the press portrayed the story as one of racial prejudice and hostility by banks toward the African American community. Overt prejudice and hostility may have been part of the story, but our longtime colleague David Messick argued that a much more common cause was likely to be in-group favoritism. That is, while there might be some overtly racist loan officers out there, the more mundane problem could be that loan officers are favoring those who resemble them, whether in terms of race, background, and so on. If predominately Caucasian loan officers are more willing to issue loans to marginally unqualified Caucasian applicants than to other applicants, the net result is that fewer funds are available for "out-groups," and the same discrimination occurs as if the loan officers were explicitly racist. This process occurs simply because loan officers are trying to be nice to members of their in-group. The punch line: in-group favoritism can have the same effects as out-group hostility, and without the discriminator thinking he has done anything wrong!

That seems to be exactly what happened at the University of Illinois for many years. In May 2009, the *Chicago Tribune* broke the story that hundreds of students with inadequate academic records were being admitted to the university because of interference from state lawmakers and university trustees.[1] From 2005 to 2009, about eight hundred applicants were admitted after receiving special consideration from high-ranking officials, according to documents obtained by the *Tribune*. Under a shadow admissions system known privately as "Category I," some underqualified applicants were admitted despite the objections of admissions officers, while others had their rejections quietly reversed. In the most publicized instance, a relative of Antoin "Tony" Rezko, who has since been convicted of influence peddling on behalf of disgraced former Illinois governor Rod Blagojevich, was admitted after University of Illinois president B. Joseph White wrote an e-mail to the university chancellor explaining that the governor wanted the applicant to be admitted. An admissions official who received the message noted that the Rezko relative had weak credentials and was about to be rejected. But the decision was reversed, and the applicant was accepted.

According to the *Tribune*'s review of documents, politically appointed university trustees and lawmakers lobbied university officials on behalf of relatives and neighbors.[2] Category I "creates an awkward situation in which university officials are taking requests from legislators who hold the school's purse strings and trustees who are, in essence, their bosses," the *Tribune* notes.[3] Most of the lawmakers involved in the scandal made their requests through the university's two top lobbyists, who have an incentive to keep lawmakers satisfied. Moreover, through one of the lobbyists, two lawmakers threatened university officials that if their candidates were not accepted, they might attempt to revamp the university's admissions system.

Notably, for the 2008–2009 school year, about 77 percent of those on the clout list were admitted to the university, as compared to 69 percent of all applicants, despite the fact that patronage candidates had significantly lower average high-school class ranks and standardized test scores than other admitted students. This policy of admitting less qualified but well-connected applicants may have had a damaging effect on the university's reputation. In 2006, Paul Pless, the dean of admissions of the University of Illinois Law School, argued that he would have to admit two additional qualified students to offset the negative impact on the school's ranking of admitting an underqualified Category I applicant. Said Pless, "When [the applicant] is faced with the rigor of our program there is absolutely no reason to expect anything other than failure."[4]

The *Chicago Tribune* exposure of Category I set off a firestorm in Illinois. In August 2009, a panel appointed by Governor Patrick Quinn issued a scathing report claiming that the university was experiencing "a full-fledged crisis of its own making" as a result of a long-term culture of "cynicism and crass opportunism."[5] High-ranking deans and officials, including President White and the university's chancellor, were accused of cooperating in the admissions of privileged, unqualified applicants, including the children of top university donors. The report called for the resignation of all members of the university's board of trustees. President White officially scrapped the Category I system and vowed to implement the panel's recommendations, including building a "firewall" to protect the admissions process from input from high-level university officials, setting up a process for fielding inquiries from lawmakers and others, and creating an admissions code of conduct. But for White, the damage was done; under intense pressure, he resigned as president in September 2009.

Given that Illinois lawmakers, University of Illinois trustees, and university officials had been unashamed of the university's admissions policy, you might wonder whether this sad story of in-group favoritism is a case of intentional corruption rather than one of implicit discrimination. The answer is both. Without a doubt, some of the wrongdoers knew they were acting unethically. But for others, a focus on helping people close to them evidently led them to overlook the fact that the university would unfairly reject some unknown individuals as a result of these actions. When questioned by the *Tribune* about their requests for favors, some lawmakers said they were just doing their job. "A constituent calls and asks for someone to help get a street paved or curb replaced or a kid get into college," a spokesperson for House Speaker Michael Madigan told the *Tribune.* "I think that's perfectly appropriate."[6] Many Illinois citizens, including some whose well-qualified children were rejected by the University of Illinois, were outraged but not entirely surprised to learn of the shadow admissions process. "If you know somebody, good things happen to you in the state of Illinois on a lot of different fronts," said Tom Wethekam, the father of a student who was rejected by the university through the usual process. "I look at this as an extension of that."[7]

Although the Category I system in Illinois stands out for its organization and size, virtually all U.S. colleges and universities field inquiries about admissions from well-connected individuals. Peter Schmidt (2007), deputy editor of the *Chronicle of Higher Education,* finds that the leading form of affirmative action at many excellent universities is "legacy admits"—the policy of admitting subpar to marginally qualified children of alumni, donors, and other well-connected individuals.[8] Legacy admission policies in elite institutions favor unqualified, less capable applicants from privileged social groups over more qualified, unconnected applicants. Most Ivy League schools fill 10–15 percent of their freshman classes with legacies.[9] Even some taxpayer-funded universities, such as the University of Virginia, have a legacy system. Officials at some universities argue that their legacy admits are just as qualified as other applicants. These statistics are difficult to verify, but one 1990 Department of Education report concluded that the typical Harvard University legacy student is "significantly less qualified" than the average nonlegacy student in every realm but sports.[10] In all likelihood, university officials, similar to the mortgage lenders who favored Caucasian borrowers, are unaware of how their policy of being "nice" to legacies discriminates against those who are not legacies.

The in-group favoritism that characterizes admissions at many U.S. universities, as well as most people's decision processes, exemplifies the core aspect of bounded ethicality: the fact that people often act unethically without their own awareness. Moreover, this form of unethical behavior is far more prevalent than intentional corruption, we believe, and requires a very different set of corrective strategies. Behavioral ethics research provides insights into how people actually make ethical decisions in comparison to how they would want to make those decisions with greater reflection. Moving beyond in-group bias, this chapter highlights other forms of bounded ethicality. We will focus on ordinary prejudice, a cousin of in-group bias, and then broaden the discussion to include two common tendencies: overclaiming credit and discounting the future.

Ordinary Prejudice

Instances of in-group favoritism illustrate how one's focus on being a good cousin, friend, neighbor, or synagogue member can result in unintentional discrimination, a type of bounded ethicality. More broadly, research from the past decade has uncovered a consistent set of preferences that people have but aren't aware they have. Amazing discoveries in the field of "implicit psychology" reveal that we have attitudes about men versus women, whites versus blacks, and, in general, "our" group versus "their" group, and that these attitudes are implicit—that is, they exist without our awareness. This work has profound implications for business, law, and medicine, and for all of us who want to truly behave ethically rather than simply view ourselves as ethical.

If you think you might be immune to unintentional discrimination, consider the story of Ashton Briggs III ("Ash"), a partner in a well-known and highly respected consulting firm. Although he was a white man from a wealthy background, he was one of his firm's most enthusiastic proponents of actively recruiting minority MBA graduates for sought-after openings in the firm. The firm's most important recruiting grounds were MBA schools. Ash successfully convinced his colleagues to make sure that underrepresented minorities made it to callbacks, which consisted of second-round, all-day interviews at the firm's offices. Despite Ash's efforts, the firm did not have a generally favorable reputation as a place for minorities to work, although the reasons for this reputation were unclear.

In the spring of 2009, fewer positions for graduating MBAs were available at Ash's firm than in the past, as at many consulting firms, because of the financial crisis that had pervaded the economy. Yet the firm continued to interview graduating MBA students with the goal of hiring a few new additions, in part to remain visible on college campuses. Ash led the company's recruiting efforts, and his team narrowed the finalists for the last available position down to two candidates.

One of the candidates had spent two years as an intern with the firm prior to getting his MBA. He had very good grades and excellent letters of recommendation. One of his letters even came from one of Ash's former professors. Prior to getting her MBA, the other finalist had spent time in the energy sector, an important industry for the consulting firm in upcoming years. Her grades were fantastic, she was the head of her MBA program's energy club, and she had one over-the-top, enthusiastic letter of recommendation from a well-known African American professor. Both candidates were obviously qualified, but only one position remained. In the end, Ash and his colleagues decided to make the offer to their former intern. A key factor was Ash's trust in the letter from his former professor, whom he recalled fondly. Although the other candidate's experience in the energy sector was valuable, the firm prized knowledge of its own systems even more.

Despite the unanimous agreement among the firm's partners, the hiring decision bothered Ash. The candidate chosen for the position was Caucasian, and the runner-up was African American. Ash had earlier instituted a policy of keeping track of the schools, gender, and race of all

applicants from MBA programs, as well as information regarding interview callbacks, offers, and acceptances. As he was filling out these forms
for the current year, Ash noticed that, firm-wide, minority applicants had
been more likely than Caucasians to get callbacks over the years, but far
less likely than Caucasians to actually get a job offer. Even more bothersome, Ash pulled up his own recommendations and learned that over the
last seven years, his pattern of recommendations matched the decisions
of the firm. He was consistently enthusiastic about bringing minorities in
for callbacks, but in the end, he seemed consistently to make tough
choices that, in the aggregate, worked against the minority candidates.

As this process was unfolding, Ash received an e-mail from a colleague referring him to a YouTube video, which was pulled from an episode of the ABC show *Dateline* (you can find a link to the video at www.
blindspots-ethics.com/dateline). The video, which featured the research
of Professors Mahzarin Banaji and Anthony Greenwald, referred viewers
to a website where over 10 million visitors have explored their implicit
preferences and received feedback about the potential ways in which
they might discriminate against others without their own awareness. In-
trigued, Ash went to the website and was presented with a computer-
based task called the Implicit Association Test. (We recommend that you
visit www.blindspots-ethics.com/implicit to see the kind of materials that
confronted Ash.) Ash was supposed to rapidly classify faces as being of
African versus European origin by pressing one of two computer keys.
He classified thirty faces in this task, which struck him as fairly trivial
and easy. Next, he was asked to classify words as good or bad. "Good,"
"peace," and "joy" were examples of good words, while "mean," "devil,"
and "awful" were examples of bad words. This task also seemed simple.

The third task asked Ash to press one key when he saw a black face or
a bad word, but to use a different key when he saw a white face or a good
word. This task was harder, but did not strain Ash's mind much.

The fourth task was similar to the third, but with a small change in
the pairings. This time, Ash was asked to press one key to judge if a face
was black or a word was good, but to press a different key when a face was

white or a word was bad. This new task sounded very similar to the prior one. This time, however, the task felt much harder, and Ash found himself making more misclassifications. Even more noticeably, in order to choose the right answer, he needed to work much more slowly than in the prior task.

The computer calculated that it had taken Ash longer to make the "black-good" and "white-bad" distinctions than to make the "black-bad" and "white-good" distinctions (as measured in milliseconds). Based on these results, the computer reported that Ash showed a moderately strong association between black and bad, and between white and good. In other words, his implicit associations revealed a preference for white over black even though he didn't have such a preference in his conscious mind.

Banaji, Greenwald, and their colleagues describe these preferences as *ordinary prejudice*. They use the word "ordinary" to highlight the fact that the ordinary thought processes humans use to categorize, perceive, and judge information can lead to systematic feelings and beliefs that can be labeled as prejudiced and stereotypical. Such thought processes can also be considered "ordinary" because they affect even very honest and smart people, including managers, executives, and other professionals. This research falls squarely in the realm of behavioral ethics.

Some scholars have questioned whether the Implicit Association Test can accurately predict actual behavior,[11] yet the IAT has led to some amazing empirical results. Researchers have found that outcomes on the IAT predict hostility to minority groups[12] and the degree to which people discriminate in selection of job candidates based on race.[13] A race-based IAT predicted differences in how Caucasians and African Americans were treated by actual medical doctors.[14] Researchers discovered the degree to which Swedes prefer to hold job interviews with other Swedes rather than Arabs.[15] In fact, there is much evidence that all groups hold a variety of implicit biases.

Now consider the media firestorm that erupted in July 2009 after President Barack Obama commented on the arrest of Henry Louis Gates Jr., an African American Harvard University professor, by James Crowley, a white Cambridge police sergeant. As you may recall, upon returning home from an overseas trip, Gates found his front door jammed and forced his way inside with the help of his cab driver. A neighbor phoned the police to report a possible break-in. Arriving at the scene, Crowley asked Gates to step outside; Gates refused. Gates says that he showed Crowley his Harvard ID card and driver's license as proof of residence, but that Crowley remained unconvinced that he lived in the home. Crowley said that while he "was led to believe" that Gates did indeed live in the home, he felt compelled to make an arrest after Gates allegedly followed Crowley onto the porch and became disorderly. At a press conference soon afterward, Obama said the Cambridge police had "acted stupidly" in arresting Gates. Debates on race ensued, culminating in a hastily arranged "beer summit" at the White House Rose Garden.

You may (or may not) agree with Obama's initial assessment that it was stupid for Crowley to arrest Gates inside his own home. More importantly, was Crowley's decision to arrest Gates a case of explicit racism? Or could Crowley have made the decision to arrest Gates without being overtly hostile to African Americans? For many Americans, it is not difficult to imagine a racist white police officer seeing criminal intent in an innocent black man's behavior and overreacting accordingly. The United States has a long, sad history of open discrimination and mistreatment of minorities by law enforcement and the courts. But James Crowley doesn't fit the profile of a racist. In fact, he teaches a course to police cadets on how to *avoid* racial profiling.

The evidence suggests that despite having been trained to treat Gates in a color-blind manner, Crowley *may* have succumbed to subconscious racial biases. In the heat of the moment, the officer had to decide how to respond to Gates. Such snap decisions are especially prone to unconscious bias; the less time we have to think, the more likely we are to fall back on racial stereotypes. In one study, participants in a computer simulation were instructed to shoot criminals, but not unarmed citizens or police officers, who appeared on the screen.[16] The participants incorrectly shot more black men than white men.[17] According to University of South

Florida criminology professor Lorie Fridell, the historical animosity between police and minorities in the United States and the widespread ste-
reotype of black men as violent and criminal can cause some police officers to expect less deference or greater aggressiveness from black men.

Most of us do not face the life-and-death decisions that police officers
do in the course of their work. Yet all of us are susceptible to making
harmful stereotypical judgments about others. If your implicit attitudes,
as measured by the IAT, are inconsistent with your conscious views, you
should at least take the results as a warning sign about the ways in which
you might discriminate without your own awareness. Banaji, who believes that "unlearning" unconscious racism requires systemic change,
also advises us to question portrayals of race in the media and to examine
our own choices of friends.[18] The less exposure we have to people who are
different from us, whether in terms of race, culture, religion, and so on,
the more likely we are to view them through a narrow, biased lens. Consider that in the aftermath of his arrest of Gates, Crowley insisted he had
acted appropriately and refused to apologize to Gates. However, Crowley
was willing to sit down with Gates (and the president and vice president)
over a beer. And when the photo opportunity had ended, the two former
adversaries met at the River Gods, a bar in Cambridge, out of the nation's
eye. This type of open communication and rational reflection can go a
long way toward minimizing the mistakes we make in the heat of the
moment.

How Egocentrism Fuels Overclaiming

No sort of scientific teaching, no kind of common interest, will ever
teach men to share property and privileges with equal consideration
for all. Everyone will think his share too small and they will be
always envying, complaining, and attacking one another.

—Fyodor Dostoyevsky, *The Brothers Karamazov*

What percentage of the housework do you do? What percentage of the good ideas in your work group come from you? What percentage of the long-term profitability of your organization can be attributed to the efforts of your division? In your firm's partnership with another firm, what percentage of the alliance's success is due to your organization's contributions?

It's impossible to know whether you "overclaimed" credit for your (or your group's) contributions when answering these questions. But research does show that most people view their own input to a group, their division's input to the overall organization, and their firm's contributions to a strategic alliance to be more important and substantial than reality can sustain. Even when people consciously try to make accurate assessments, they still overclaim credit. This overclaiming is at least partly rooted in our bounded ethicality.

Academics have been found guilty of succumbing to this phenomenon. Consider the co-winners of the 1923 Nobel Prize for the discovery of insulin. One of the winners, Frederick Banting, argued that his partner, John Macleod, who was the head of their laboratory, was more of a hindrance than a help. For his part, in speeches describing the research that led to the discovery, Macleod somehow forget to mention that he had a partner.[19] More recently, Max and his colleagues Eugene Caruso and Nick Epley asked authors of four-author articles in the field of organizational behavior to distribute credit for work done on their articles. On average, the sum of the credit that each group member claimed for himself or herself added up to 140 percent. We don't know whether all four members of a given group overclaimed credit, only that the four people collectively claimed 40 percent more credit than they deserved. As a result of such honest overclaiming (honest because each person believes his or her estimate is accurate), it becomes impossible for all or even most of the authors involved to feel they were given appropriate credit by the group for the work they performed. Worse, conflict can erupt when each member seeks the credit (e.g., order of authorship) she believes she deserves.

In the midst of disagreements, we often fail to see eye to eye. Why? Because different people are paying attention to different data. The tendency to focus on your own contributions to a joint effort and not on those of other group members reflects another widespread bias with an ethical dimension: egocentrism. It's in our nature to be egocentric—that is, to make self-serving judgments regarding allocations of credit and blame, a phenomenon that in turn leads us to different conclusions regarding what a fair solution to a problem would be. Specifically, we tend to first determine our preference for a certain outcome on the basis of self-interest, and then justify this preference on the basis of fairness by altering the importance of the attributes that affect what is fair.[20]

Consider what happens when a defendant and a litigant in a labor dispute are presented with identical information. Both parties process the information differently and in a way that supports their own perspective, researchers have found.[21] As compared to the plaintiffs, defendants remember more details that support their case and don't remember details that support the plaintiff's case. The reverse phenomenon occurs for plaintiffs. The tendency to view the situation from a self-serving perspective affects parties' perceptions of what constitutes a fair settlement; similarly, the level of disagreement between labor and management in contract disputes about what is fair predicts the length of a labor strike.

This difference in the way information is processed isn't just strategic; it happens whether we want it to or not. Our minds actually absorb the information that is advantageous to us and ignore information that isn't. No wonder, then, that most people facing a court case or an arbitration hearing overestimate the likelihood that they will prevail.[22] They can't be right, of course; each side can't have, say, a 75 percent chance of winning. But according to the facts they choose to see, both sides believe they are in the right. The problem is that the "facts" they rely on for their estimates are biased in a way that favors a win. Missing are those facts that don't support their case.

Similarly, in another study, students in a negotiation class were given diverse materials (depositions, medical and police reports, etc.) from a

stead focused on Locke's acknowledgment that the United States had been emitting greenhouse gases for 150 years.

The U.S. government may indeed desire a climate change agreement that is fair to both the United States and China, but its view of what is fair is likely biased by self-interest—and the same is bound to be true for China. Unfortunately, egocentrism leads all nations to believe they honestly deserve less responsibility for reversing climate change than an independent party would judge to be fair. The problem is exacerbated not by our desire to be unfair but by our inability to view information objectively. Moreover, climate change is a highly complex issue that lacks conclusive scientific and technological data. This uncertainty allows egocentrism to run rampant. When data are clear, the mind's ability to manipulate fairness is limited; under extreme uncertainty, egocentrism is strongly exacerbated.

Overfishing is another example of a widespread and intractable social dilemma rooted in egocentrism. Because fish that populate the high seas can be caught by anyone, they are especially susceptible to being depleted. Take the case of bluefin tuna, a species that has been decimated by overfishing. Currently the most valuable fish in the ocean, bluefin tuna grow up to ten feet in length and weigh up to 1,500 pounds. In Tokyo, a single bluefin tuna can fetch up to $150,000.

Back in 1969, when abundant stocks of bluefin roamed the North, Baltic, and Mediterranean seas, one of the first regional, intergovernmental fisheries-management organizations was formed to oversee bluefin tuna conservation: the Madrid-based International Commission for the Conservation of Atlantic Tunas (ICCAT). Nonetheless, in the decades that followed, stocks of bluefin tuna plummeted. One recent study concluded that even if the fishing of bluefin tuna were banned entirely, the northeast Atlantic and Mediterranean populations would probably collapse nonetheless.[27] In recent years, ICCAT has set fishing quotas of about 30,000 tons of bluefin tuna per year, with a plan to lower quotas to 25,500 in the near future. Yet legal catches of the fish are poorly monitored, and illegal fishing of bluefin tuna thrives.

ICCAT has done such a poor job of managing bluefin tuna stocks that some joke the group's acronym stands for "International Conspiracy to Catch All Tunas." Indeed, an outside review panel of experts appointed by ICCAT said the fishery group's management of bluefin tuna was "widely regarded as an international disgrace."[28] Why has ICCAT been so ineffective at meeting its mission? Because the ICCAT exerts little control over its forty-six member states, leaving their egocentrism unchecked.[29] A solution to the problem lies, at least in part, in recognizing the stronghold that egocentrism exerts on ICCAT members' decisions. Given the unrecognized strong influence of this bias, we cannot expect individual fishers to voluntarily commit to reducing their catch in the name of the common good. Rather, changes are needed at the system level.

In September 2008, at a meeting of the International Union for Conservation of Nature, most countries signed a resolution calling for a moratorium on bluefin tuna fishing, followed by better management and enforcement measures. But after the resolution was signed, governments began backing away from their promises. A spokesperson for the European Union's fisheries directorate complained that a moratorium on bluefin tuna fishing would mean "despair for Italian, Spanish, and French fishermen."[30] It is easy to feel sympathy for fishers who will lose their livelihood if tighter fishing quotas are enforced or a total ban on bluefin tuna fishing is put in place. But if the fishery had been effectively managed over the past forty years, fishers could continue to fish without fear of a moratorium. Moreover, for bluefin tuna fishers to have any hope of rebuilding a sustainable fishery for their children and grandchildren, they may need to stop fishing tuna and allow stocks to rebuild. But unsustainable harvesting continues.[31]

The slow extinction of bluefin tuna is just one of many stories of fishery decline and depletion. Throughout the high seas, too many high-tech boats and factory trawlers are chasing after ever-dwindling species of fish. Fishers have wiped out entire fish populations, only to move on to less attractive species of fish. As is the case in the majority of fishing basins throughout the world, cod and haddock were dramatically overfished in the northeastern United States, and shark was overfished off the south-east U.S. coast. Unfortunately, fishers often become interested in solving an overfishing crisis too late in the game. Consistent with other biases within the field of behavioral ethics, this overclaiming occurs without any individual group member realizing that its behavior has ethical consequences. In fact, much of the problem can be traced to different fishing groups believing they are only pursuing their fair share. Yet fishers suffer greatly in the long run from their short-term overclaiming. When Canada was forced to close its cod fishery in 1993, 40,000 jobs were lost. And currently, eleven of the world's fifteen major fishing regions and about 70 percent of the most desirable fish species are in decline.[32]

Motivated by this worldwide catastrophe, we created a simulation with Kimberly Wade-Benzoni of Duke University based on the real-life crisis that existed in the 1980s in the northeastern U.S. fishery, back when there was still time to save this fishing basin.[33] The simulation described a conference consisting of four representatives from various commercial and recreational fishing groups. Participants were divided into groups of four, and each participant was assigned to represent one of the four fishing groups. The four fishing groups differed in the degree to which they would benefit from conservation, but collectively, they were better off reducing their harvests by half in order to be able to continue to fish in the future.

Each participant read an overview of the data on the fishing crisis, then gathered with their four-person group for a nonbinding, thirty-minute discussion. Next, we asked each participant to tell us, confidentially, what they perceived the fair allocation of harvesting to be among the four fishing groups, and then to tell us the amount of fish they would harvest over the next year. For each participant, we calculated the percentage of the future harvest the participant believed would be fair for his fishing group to claim. We found (and these results have since been replicated many times) that self-serving interpretations of fairness existed: the sum of the four percentages far exceeded 100 percent. Further, these self-serving interpretations were an excellent predictor of overharvesting in the simulation.

These experimental results suggest that real-world fishing crises and other instances of overclaiming may occur because honest people are egocentric and therefore have honestly different views of what is fair. If this is true, they will not recognize when they make an unfair claim. Creating awareness of the natural tendency to be egocentric and overclaim credit offers a productive focus for solutions to current environmental crises. In fact, teaching individuals about the insidious influence of egocentrism has been shown to be effective at teaching them to recognize the egocentrism of others.[34] Thus, before you accuse someone of being selfish, first try to consider the matter from her perspective. Ask yourself if she believes she deserves what she is claiming. Employers, for example, would be wise to spend some time thinking about an employee's sense of self-worth before opening a discussion of the employee's bonus.

Unfortunately, such training on egocentrism doesn't reduce the influence of egocentrism on our own behavior. While we recognize that others are egocentric, we don't believe the bias affects us—an egocentric interpretation of the egocentric bias! To compensate for this problem, some advice offered by philosopher John Rawls proves useful. Rawls proposes that fairness should be assessed under a "veil of ignorance"—that is, we ideally should judge a situation without knowing the role we ourselves play in it. So, when dividing up a pie, one person should be the "pie slicer" and the other should be the first to take a slice.

Overly Discounting the Future

Would you prefer to receive $1,000 today or $1,180 a year from now? In controlled experiments, many people choose the former, despite having the opportunity to earn an 18 percent return on their investment. Similarly, homeowners too often fail to insulate their homes appropriately and fail to purchase energy-efficient appliances and fluorescent lighting, even when the payback would be extremely quick and the rate of return far greater than the 18 percent in the problem above. As these anecdotes illustrate, we all too often use an extremely high discounting rate regarding the future. We tend to focus on or overweight short-term considerations at the expense of long-term concerns.[35] As a result of this pattern, too many people save far too little for retirement, creating a personal crisis for themselves and for their families.[36]

The tendency to ignore the future consequences of our actions played out in dramatic fashion in the U.S. housing crisis that began in 2006 and ignited the financial collapse of 2008–2009. During the real-estate bubble, developers and lenders did a booming business that involved building more and more homes and offering home loans to more and more people. Low-income citizens who previously had only dreamed of owning their own home suddenly found themselves courted by real-estate brokers offering low-interest, adjustable rate mortgages (ARMs). In the past, homebuyers had to make a substantial down payment and prove to lenders that they earned enough income to afford their monthly mortgage payments for the next fifteen or thirty years. But as the housing bubble expanded, lenders began to lower their standards. Income requirements relaxed. Eventually, some lenders stopped requiring any proof of income at all. Suddenly, it seemed as if every potential "subprime borrower" was taking out an ARM to finance his or her dream home.

Of course, the recipients of these loans should have paused to consider what would happen when their ARMs exploded after three, five, or seven years. Yet few of them did. Overdiscounting the future, they focused narrowly on their low introductory payments. But when the housing bubble began to burst, housing prices fell, interest rates rose, and refinancing became more difficult. For the subprime borrowers who could not afford the new rates on their ARMs, the inevitable result was an epidemic of mortgage delinquencies and foreclosures. Of course, lenders, blinded by the sky-high profits they gained from bundling and selling off subprime loans, are also to blame for failing to anticipate the consequences of handing out loans to unqualified applicants.

The tendency to overly discount the future is not limited to individuals; organizations also are susceptible. One Ivy League university completed a major renovation of its infrastructure without using the most cost-efficient products from a long-term perspective.[37] University administrators knew that this decision was a long-term mistake. But because of capital constraints on construction, the university implicitly placed a very high discount rate on construction decisions, emphasizing reduction in its capital costs over the long-term costs of running the building. In the process, the university passed on returns that its financial office would have been thrilled to receive on its investments. In addition, the university was less environmentally friendly than its claims about its future building plans suggested. Collectively, the university's inconsistent discount rate led administrators to destroy value. In contrast, as part of its Green Campus Initiative, Harvard University has set up a fund to finance environmental sustainability projects for different colleges within the university that may have been overlooked because of short-term budget pressures. This initiative reduces the likelihood that university units will make poor long-term decisions as a result of the tendency to overly discount the future. Given the financial disaster that hit Harvard and other universities in 2008, these environmental initiatives turned out to be some of the best investments made by the university.

When an individual or organization applies an inappropriately high discount rate to decisions, behavioral decision researchers tend to treat these mistakes as decision errors. Yet we argue that when others suffer because of a decision and future generations are forced to pay for our mistakes, the problem becomes an ethical issue. Overdiscounting the future is not only foolish, but also immoral, as it robs future generations of opportunities and resources. But many people, organizations, and nations commit these mistakes without any awareness that their behavior is ethically bounded and, in many cases, unethical as a result. When people claim they want to treat the earth with respect, they generally are thinking about their own descendants. But when the time comes to make investments for future generations by reducing our own standards of living, we begin to view future generations as too vague to be fully considered in our choices.

At a societal level, the problems brought about by overdiscounting the future can be severe. Inappropriately high discount rates lead to a broad array of environmental problems, including the ocean overharvesting we discussed previously and the failure to invest in new technologies to respond to climate change. Herman Daly observes that we often make environmental decisions as if the earth "were a business in liquidation."[38] We discount the future the most when it is uncertain and distant and when intergenerational distribution of resources is involved.[39] Discounting of the future leads to species extinction, the melting of polar ice caps, uranium leaks, and hazardous waste contamination.

The unintentionally unethical behavior that results from overdiscounting the future is not just an environmental issue. It also helps to explain the massive size of the national debt in the United States and in many other countries in the world. As the baby boomer generation nears retirement, the United States will face ever-rising entitlement costs. An aging population, longer life expectancy, and rising health-care costs will combine to make Social Security, Medicare, and Medicaid costs climb sky high by 2030. At the same time, the ratio of retirees to workers is expected to have doubled between 2000 and 2030. Fewer workers will be contributing taxes to pay for the expenses of millions of elderly Americans.

Republicans typically fight against new taxes and cuts in defense spending, while Democrats resist cuts to social services. Both sides believe they are defending ethical principles. Yet they both pursue their political agenda while collectively ignoring the unethical financial mess they are leaving for future generations. For example, consider President George W. Bush's plan to subsidize the costs of prescription drugs for the elderly. When the plan went into effect on January 1, 2006, it was so convoluted that most Medicare beneficiaries could not figure out how to sign up for it, and many more were unable to receive their prescriptions at the promised discounted prices. The plan's design prohibits the government from negotiating drug prices with pharmaceutical companies, as it does in other federal health programs—a design "flaw" that benefits the insurance companies at the expense of taxpayers and retirees. The much-reviled "Medicare D" plan was projected to cost more than $1 trillion in the first ten years of its existence and contributed sizably to the $1.3 trillion deficit facing the country at the end of the Bush administration. Yet, due to the power of special-interest groups, the Democrats did little to eliminate this ill-conceived plan, even after winning control of the executive and legislative branches of government in 2009.

In this chapter, we explored the range of ethical lapses that may be created by bounded ethicality. Specifically, we examined situations within the field of behavioral ethics in which decision makers commonly engage in unethical behavior without realizing they are doing so. Having described the nature of these errors, in the next chapter we will consider why smart, honest people engage in these behaviors and, as a consequence, are less ethical than they think they are.

Chapter 4

Why You Aren't as Ethical as You Think You Are

In chapter 1, we asked you to rate your ethics in comparison to others. We have asked groups of executives attending negotiation classes to answer similar questions, such as whether they are less honest than their peers, just as honest as their peers, or more honest than their peers. As you would now expect, an overwhelming majority tell us they believe they are more honest than most others in their class.

Now consider a recent survey of high school students.[1] Nearly two-thirds of teens surveyed reported cheating on a test during the past year. More than a third admitted to plagiarizing off the Internet, nearly a third admitted to stealing from a store in the past year, and more than 80 percent said they had lied to a parent about something significant. Yet 93 percent of these high school students said they were satisfied with their ethical character.

As behavioral ethics research would predict, some of the most spectacular ethical scandals of recent years have involved people who insisted they were more ethical than their alleged actions suggested. Kenneth Lay, CEO of Enron, repeatedly insisted he had done nothing wrong during his tenure at the disgraced corporation. Bill Clinton told the American public—and perhaps rationalized to himself—that he didn't have sexual relations with Monica Lewinsky. And after Rod Blagojevich, the former governor of Illinois, was accused of trying to sell Barack Obama's vacated Senate seat to the highest bidder, he insisted he was innocent in the face of mounting evidence.

Several explanations might explain such claims of ethicality and denials of wrongdoing in the face of clearly dishonest behavior. First, it may be that the person truly is innocent; if only we had access to all the information that he does, we would agree with his assessment of his ethical character. Second, it is possible that the person doesn't actually believe he behaved ethically, but rather claims to be ethical to reduce the damages associated with his unethical actions. The third—and, we argue, most likely—explanation is also the most troubling in terms of improving one's behavior. It is possible that the person inherently believes in his own ethicality, despite the evidence to the contrary.

You may never have been accused of setting up fictitious corporate partnerships in order to steal money from investors, having relations with interns, or selling a Senate seat. Yet the chances are good that you, like Lay, Clinton, and Blagojevich (and like us), also believe you are more ethical than you really are and than others judge you to be. Behavioral ethics research suggests that biases in our thought processes make these illusions about our ethicality possible. Along with our colleagues Kristina Diekmann and Kimberly Wade-Benzoni, we argue that these biases occur at several stages of the decision-making process.[2] Prior to being faced with an ethical dilemma, people predict that they will make an ethical choice. When actually faced with an ethical dilemma, they make an unethical choice. Yet when reflecting back on that decision, they believe they are still ethical people. Together, this culminating set of biases leads to erroneously positive perceptions of our own ethicality. Worse yet, it prevents us from seeing the need to improve our ethicality, and so the pattern repeats itself.

In this chapter, we focus on the psychological processes that behavioral ethicists have identified as preventing people from making ethical decisions at these three stages—before, during, and after a moral decision.

Before You Make the Decision: Prediction Errors

Imagine that a young female college student is seeking on-campus employment to supplement her living expenses. She sees a help-wanted ad posted on campus for a research assistant. The hours and pay are just what she's looking for, so she immediately applies for the position. She is called in for an interview and meets with a man who appears to be in his early thirties. During the course of the interview, he asks her a number of standard interview questions, as well as the following three questions:

Do you have a boyfriend?
Do people find you desirable?
Do you think it is appropriate for women to wear bras to work?

What do you think the young woman would do in this situation? If you think she would feel outraged and confront the interviewer about his inappropriate questions, you are not alone. A research study examined this exact situation.[3] When asked to predict how they would behave in such an interview, 62 percent of female college students said they would ask the interviewer why he was asking these questions or tell him that the questions were inappropriate, and 68 percent said they would refuse to answer the questions.

These students' predictions may be unsurprising, yet they aren't accurate. In the same study, the researchers put female college students in the same interview situation described above. A thirty-two-year-old male interviewer actually asked them the offensive questions. What happened? *None* of the students refused to answer the questions. A minority, not a majority, did ask the interviewer why the questions had been asked, but they did so politely and usually at the end of the interview.

The human tendency to make inaccurate predictions about our own behavior is well documented by behavioral ethics and other research.[4] We firmly believe we will behave a certain way in a given situation. When actually faced with that situation, however, we behave differently. Examples of such "behavioral forecasting errors" abound. We aren't very good at predicting how often we will go the dentist. We are lousy at estimating how long it will take us to complete a particular task at work or a project at home. We underestimate the extent to which we'll be influenced by pressure from a boss or a peer. New Year's resolutions are the epitome of behavioral forecasting errors. At the beginning of the year, we set expectations of ourselves for certain behaviors, including those in the moral domain. We even expend resources to "make sure" we meet our goals. We join health clubs, hire personal trainers, or buy clothes that are too small for us. We vow to be more patient, do volunteer work in our free time, or find ways to conserve energy. We believe that in the coming year, we will be a "new" person. Come December 31, we find that little has changed—yet we make the same predictions about our behavior for the following year.

Now consider the fact that when patients are diagnosed with an illness, they are sometimes presented with the choice to participate in a clinical trial. Clinical trials are used to evaluate the effectiveness of treatments for a particular disease or to assess the safety of medications. Patients involved in a clinical trial are divided into groups, and each group receives a different treatment. At the end of the trial, the effectiveness of each treatment is measured, including its impact on the disease and whether it came with side effects. Patients and their families are often presented with the question, "Do you want to participate in a clinical trial?"

The decision to participate in clinical trials is often a *social dilemma*. As we explained in chapter 3, social dilemmas are situations in which a group's interests conflict with the interests of the group's individual members. For example, people who believe in the societal benefits of conserving fuel may nonetheless choose to drive rather than walk, using the justification that "my car's emissions won't really make a difference." Social dilemmas lie at the heart of many intractable problems, including environmental conservation, nuclear disarmament, and even group projects at work. In social dilemmas, the easiest individual strategy is to "defect"—to harvest fish that are near extinction, consume fuel, maintain a nuclear stockpile, or slack in your efforts. Yet when individual members defect, the group goal—whether preserving certain species, creating environmental improvements, making a safer world, or completing a project—is often sacrificed. In these cases, if everyone cooperated just a little bit, a lot could be achieved for the broader group. Yet for the individual, pursuing one's self-interest appears to be the most rational goal.

The decision of whether to participate in a clinical trial is a type of social dilemma because it requires individuals to cooperate in order to help others in the future. Participation does not necessarily improve patients' outcomes; patients may receive a treatment in a clinical trial that is not only unproven, but possibly not as good as currently available treatments. Many clinical trials are most likely to benefit people who will receive new and better treatments in the future, rather than those who are sick in the present. Moreover, the benefits and costs to the current patient are typically unclear and very hard to assess. The ultimate goal of clinical trials is to improve the quality of medicine so that everyone will eventually receive better treatments and a better prognosis.

Suppose that as you think about the decision to participate in a clinical trial and predict how you would behave, you come to the conclusion that everyone who is qualified should participate in clinical trials when offered the chance. You believe that the "right" choice to make is to contribute to the greater good of advances in medicine and that everyone, including yourself, should do the same. As a result of such thinking, you predict that you would certainly choose to engage yourself or a family member in a clinical trial if the occasion ever arose.

Now fast-forward a number of years and imagine that your child has been diagnosed with a life-threatening illness. Depending on how your child responds to the latest treatment, the prognosis for your child's five-year survival is between 75 and 95 percent. You have researched your child's disease to some extent and know that the newest approved treatment has demonstrated significantly positive results.

As you are discussing your child's disease, the doctor asks whether you would agree to place your child in a clinical trial in which a computer would determine which treatment your child will receive. When you ask the doctor about the comparative efficacy of the two treatments, she tells you that the new treatment is too early in its development for her to be able to answer the question. Are you willing to give up the known, approved treatment for a risky option in which the likely outcome is unknown? Your answer is quick and unwavering: No!

All of us can relate to this type of dramatic about-face. When a decision about your child's health is purely theoretical, you have the luxury of carefully deliberating and making the decision that is most compatible with your ethics. But if such a decision ever becomes a reality, your ethical considerations related to the greater good are likely to go out the window. Now all that matters is your own child and what is best for her. In the next section, we explain why such behavioral forecasting errors occur.

Decision Time: The Want Self Rears Its Head

Social scientists have long argued that we often experience conflict within ourselves. The most common form of such conflict occurs between the "want self" and the "should self."[5] The want self describes the side of you that's emotional, affective, impulsive, and hot-headed. In contrast, your should self is rational, cognitive, thoughtful, and cool-headed. The should self encompasses our ethical intentions and the belief that we should behave according to our ethical values and principles. By contrast, the want self reflects our actual behavior, which is typically characterized by self-interest and a relative disregard for ethical considerations.

Our research suggests that whether the want self or the should self dominates varies across time. The should self dominates before and after we make a decision, but the want self often wins at the moment of decision. Thus, when approaching a decision, we predict that we will make the decision we think we should make. We think we should confront a sexually harassing interviewer; therefore, we predict we will stand up to one during an interview. We think we should go to the dentist, do our share of the work at home or at the office, stand up to peer pressure, exercise, and eat healthy foods. We think we should cooperate in social dilemmas, even at a personal cost, for the sake of the greater good. In sum, we predict we will make "should decisions," or those based on our principles and ethical ideals. But at launch time, when we actually make the decision, something entirely different happens.

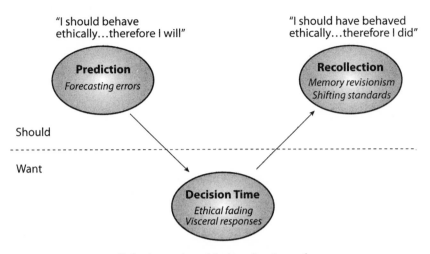

"I should behave
ethically...therefore I will"

Prediction
Forecasting errors

"I should have behaved
ethically...therefore I did"

Recollection
Memory revisionism
Shifting standards

Should

Want

Decision Time
Ethical fading
Visceral responses

"I don't see the ethical implications of
this decision . . . so I do what I want to do"

Figure 5. A temporal perspective on the battle between our "want" and "should"
selves

When it comes time to make a decision, our thoughts are dominated
by thoughts of how we *want* to behave; thoughts of how we *should* behave
disappear. A study of movie rental preferences vividly demonstrates the
dominance of the want self at the time of a decision.[6] Consider that we
tend to categorize movies we haven't seen into two basic types: educational or artistic movies that we think we should watch, such as *90 Degrees
South: With Scott to the Antarctic*, and movies we actually want to watch,
such as *Kill Bill 2*. In Max's study with Katy Milkman and Todd Rogers,
people returned "want" movies to an online DVD rental company significantly earlier than they returned "should" movies, suggesting that the
"should" DVDs sat unwatched on coffee tables longer than the "want"
movies did. At the time study participants actually decided which movie
to watch, the "want" self beat the "should" self.

When ordering movies to watch later, we are in the prediction phase
of decision making, forecasting which movies we think we will watch. At
this time, we are preoccupied by thoughts of what we *should* watch. An
internal dialogue might go something like this: "If I'm going to sit in

front of the screen doing nothing, the very least I can do is watch something educational." The should self dominates, and you order an educational, "should watch" movie along with more entertaining fare. At the moment you actually decide which movie to watch, however, the thought of educating yourself is farthest from your mind. Your pragmatic, hotheaded, self-interested want self overwhelms the rational, cool-headed should self, and you decide to veg out in front of *Kill Bill 2* (or a mindless comedy, if *Kill Bill 2* isn't your taste).

How does this reasoning apply to ethical decisions? When considering the behavior of those involved in recent scandals, such as Bernard Madoff or Rod Blagojevich, most of us firmly believe we never would have engaged in such behaviors, would not have supported such behaviors if told to do so, and would have reported any wrongdoing we saw. We believe we would behave as we think we *should* behave—according to our morals, ideals, and principles. Yet too often, behavioral ethics research shows that when presented with a decision with an ethical dimension, we behave differently than our predictions of how we would behave. Our want self wins out, and unethical behavior ensues.

Why do we predict we will behave one way and then behave another way, over and over again throughout our lives? Social scientists have discovered that we think about a decision quite differently when we are predicting how we will behave than when we have to act, a difference that is driven both by different motivations at these two points in time and by the process of ethical fading. When we think about our future behavior, it is difficult to anticipate the actual situation we will face. General principles and attitudes drive our predictions; we see the forest but not the trees. As the situation approaches, however, we begin to see the trees, and the forest disappears. Our behavior is driven by details, not abstract principles.

Consider a study of charitable contributions to the American Cancer Society's "Daffodil Days." More than 80 percent of participants who were asked if they would buy a daffodil to make a contribution predicted they would do so.[7] In fact, when actually faced with this decision, only about half of study participants who said they would buy a daffodil actually did. Clearly, they thought about the general benefits of supporting a good cause and their motivation to do so, without thinking about what might influence them at the time they are asked to donate, such as time and money constraints or distractions. At the time of the actual decision, they may have found themselves faced with pragmatic issues, such as the need to buy lunch and a limited amount of money in their pockets, details that did not cross their mind when they were predicting how they would behave. They weighed buying a daffodil against buying lunch, and lunch won.

One of the reasons we think differently about a situation when we are predicting our behavior than when we are making an actual decision is that our motivations aren't the same at these two points in time. In a study of negotiation behavior, negotiators predicted that if they were faced with a competitive opponent, they would fight fire with fire and behave competitively themselves.[8] When actually faced with a competitive opponent, however, negotiators became *less* aggressive, not more. This difference between predicted and actual behavior was traced to differences in motivations at these two points in time. When thinking about how they would behave when faced with a competitive opponent, negotiators were motivated to "win" and to prevent someone from taking advantage of them. When actually negotiating, negotiators were instead motivated simply to get a deal and avoid walking away with nothing. Similarly, the average person's motivation when predicting whether to enroll one's child in a clinical trial centers on benefiting society; at the time of the decision, however, the motivation focuses on one's own child.

When decisions have an ethical dimension, Ann's research with David Messick shows that ethical fading may also be a key factor driving the difference between how we think we will behave and how we actually behave.[9] In the prediction phase, we may clearly see the ethical aspect of a given decision. Our moral values are evoked, and we believe we will behave according to those values. As discussed in chapter 2, models of ethical decision making derived by philosophers, in fact, often predict that moral awareness will prompt moral behavior.[10] However, at the time of the decision, ethical fading occurs, and we no longer see the ethical dimension of a decision. Instead, we might be preoccupied with making the best business or legal decision. Ethical principles don't appear to be relevant, so they don't enter into our decision, and we behave unethically as a result.

The story of the Ford Pinto, an infamous case from the 1970s, illustrates how ethical fading at the time of the decision can lead to disastrous results. In the case of rear-end collisions, the Pinto's gas tank was found to explode at an unacceptable frequency. And because the car's doors jammed up during accidents, numerous people died in Pinto accidents in the 1970s.

In the aftermath of the scandal, the decision process that led to the Pinto's faulty design was scrutinized. Under intense competition from Volkswagen, Ford had rushed the Pinto into production in a significantly shorter time period than was usually the case. The potential danger of ruptured fuel tanks was discovered in preproduction crash tests, but with the assembly line ready to go, the decision was made to manufacture the car anyway. This decision was based on a cost-benefit analysis that weighed the minimal cost of repairing the flaw (about $11 per vehicle at the time) against the cost of paying off potential lawsuits following accidents. Ford deemed it would be cheaper to pay off lawsuits than to make the repair. The Pinto was manufactured with its faulty design for eight more years.

We suspect that none of the Ford executives who were involved in this now-notorious decision would have predicted in advance that they would make such an unethical choice. Nonetheless, they made a choice that maimed and killed many people. Why? It appears that, at the time of the decision, they viewed it as a "business decision" rather than an "ethical decision." Taking an approach heralded as "rational" in most business-school curriculums, the executives conducted a cost-benefit analysis that provided a lens through which they viewed and made the decision. Ethics faded from the decision; the moral dimensions of injuries and deaths were not part of the equation. Because the calculations suggested that producing the car without redesign was the best business decision, the dangerous fuel tank remained.

What causes ethical fading? Our body's innate needs may be partly to blame. Visceral responses dominate at the time we make decisions.[11] Such mechanisms are hardwired into our brains to increase our chances of survival. Hunger, for example, is a message that our body needs nourishment. Pain signals that we may be facing danger in our environment. Our behavior in such situations becomes automatic, geared toward addressing the messages from our brain. Our responses to such influences take over at the time of the decision to ensure our chances of survival.

Such mechanisms obviously provide valuable information that can guide us toward necessary behaviors, such as eating to nourish ourselves or fleeing danger. But our visceral responses can also be counterproductive in other domains. Suppose you decide to wake up early tomorrow to get a head start on cutting down your to-do list. You set your alarm for 5:30 A.M. with every intention of waking up early. When the alarm goes off, however, the desire to get more sleep overwhelms all other considerations. You turn off the alarm and go back to sleep. At the time of the decision, visceral responses lead to an inward focus dominated by short-term gains. We direct our attention toward satisfying our innate needs, which are driven by self-preservation. Other goals, such as concern for others' interests and even our own long-term interests, vanish. In the case of the Pinto fuel tank decision, the pressures of competition likely produced feelings akin to the survival instinct: Avoiding market loss, getting a big bonus, and "looking good" within the company became the sole goals of the Ford executives at the time of the decision. Ethical considerations faded away.

And, as noted earlier, when we face ethical dilemmas, our actions often precede reasoning. In other words, we make quick decisions based on fleeting feelings rather than on carefully calculated reasoning. Our visceral responses are so dominant at the time of the decision that they overshadow all other considerations. We want to help our company maintain its market share. We want to earn profits and bonuses. As a result, want wins, and should loses. It is only later, behavioral ethics researchers argue, that we engage in any type of moral reasoning. The purpose of this moral reasoning is not to arrive at a decision—it's too late for that—but to justify the decisions we have already made.

Postdecision: Recollection Biases

As we gain distance from our visceral responses to an ethical dilemma, the ethical implications of our choices come back into full color. We are faced with a contradiction between our beliefs about ourselves as ethical people and our unethical actions. This type of discrepancy is unsettling, to say the least, and we are likely to be motivated to reduce the dissonance that results. So strong is the need to do so that researchers found in one study that offering people an opportunity to wash their hands after behaving immorally reduced their need to compensate for an immoral action (for example, by volunteering to help someone).[12] In this study, the opportunity to cleanse oneself of an immoral action—in this case, physically—was sufficient to restore one's self-image; no other action was needed.

Individuals can also restore their self-image through psychological cleansing.[13] Psychological cleansing is an aspect of moral disengagement, a process that allows us to selectively turn our usual ethical standards on and off at will. For example, Neeru Paharia and Rohit Deshpandé have found that consumers who desire an article of clothing that they know was produced with child labor reconcile their push-pull attraction to the purchase by reducing the degree to which they view child labor as a societal problem.[14] Similarly, Max's work with Lisa Shu and Francesca Gino shows that when people are in environments that allow them to cheat, they reduce the degree to which they view cheating as morally problematic.[15] The process of moral disengagement allows us to behave contrary to our personal code of ethics, while still maintaining the belief that we are ethical people.

Psychological cleansing can take different forms. Just as our predictions of how we will respond to an ethical dilemma diverge from how we behave in the heat of the moment, our recollections of our behavior don't match our thoughts at the actual time of the decision. Our memory is selective; specifically, we remember behaviors that support our self-image and conveniently forget those that do not. We rationalize unethical behavior, change our definition of ethical behavior, and, over time, become desensitized to our own unethical behavior.

Reflecting back on their high school or college days, most people remember an easygoing lifestyle, laughter, fun, and excitement. They may not remember specific conversations or what they did on a daily basis, but their recollections are probably vaguely positive. Most likely, they had very different perceptions of their lives when they were actually attending high school or college. They probably have forgotten the specifics, such as getting up early for an 8:00 A.M. class, suffering through four finals in two days, or obsessing about a boyfriend or girlfriend who failed to call. Similarly, when we reflect on the ethicality of our past behavior, we focus on abstract principles, not the small details of our actions—the forest, not the trees. Instead of thinking about a particular lie that you told or a particular misstatement in your finances, you are likely to think abstractly about your general behavior and to conclude from this perspective that you generally act according to your ethical principles.

Our inflated view of our own ethicality is also enabled by our tendency to become "revisionist historians." After making the decision not to enroll your sick child in a clinical trial but instead to make sure your child receives the best treatment available, you quickly reformulate that decision as an example of your competence and diligence in examining and assessing the available medical options. Self-serving biases are responsible for such revisionist impulses. As we discussed in chapter 3, two people can look at the same situation very differently, reflecting on what is advantageous to themselves and forgetting or never "coding" that which is not. When we recall our past behavior, these self-serving biases help to hide our unethical actions. The implicit goal is not to arrive at an accurate picture of ourselves, but rather to create a picture that fits with our desired self-view.

If we do remember details, we focus on times when we told the truth or stood up for our principles; meanwhile, we forget the lies we told or the times when we bowed under pressure. Upon looking back at a particular job negotiation, for instance, an applicant might remember that she told the interviewer the truth about where she wanted to live and whether she would be willing to relocate, but conveniently forgot that she lied about how much she was currently earning. Because we are motivated by a desire to see ourselves as ethical people, we remember the actions and decisions that were ethical and forget, or never even process, those that were not, thereby leaving intact our image of ourselves as ethical.

But our self-serving biases are not completely foolproof. Occasionally, we might actually "see" that, yes, perhaps we did behave unethically in a given situation. Typically, however, we find ways to internally "spin" this behavior, whether by rationalizing our role, changing our definition of what's ethical, or casting unethical actions in a more positive light. Bill Clinton argued that he didn't have "sexual relations" with Monica Lewinsky, a lie that he might have justified by changing the standard definition of "sexual relations" in his mind. Similarly, accountants might decide that they engaged in "creative accounting" rather than broke the law.

We are also experts at deflecting blame. Psychologists have long known that we like to blame other people and other things for our failures and take personal credit for our successes. We are able to maintain a positive self-image when we blame problems on influences outside of our control—whether the economy, a boss, or a family member—and take personal credit for all that has gone well thanks to our intelligence, intuition, or personality. A used-car salesman can view himself as ethical, despite selling someone a car that leaks oil, by noting that the potential buyer didn't ask the right questions. Guards responsible for carrying out the death penalty rationalize their actions by placing responsibility on the legal system: "I'm just following the law." And when caught engaging in unethical but legal acts, many people working in business environments are quick to note that the law permits their behavior and that they are maximizing shareholder value.

The hierarchies found in most organizations provide a built-in source of blame: one's boss. Do any of these phrases sound familiar? "I'm just doing my job." "Ask the boss, not me." "I just follow orders." The reverse is also true; bosses face strong temptations to blame their employees for unethical behavior and claim personal innocence. Kenneth Lay rationalized his unethical actions at Enron by blaming Andrew Fastow, the firm's chief financial officer. Lay argued that Fastow misled him and Enron's board of directors about the off-the-book partnerships that eventually led to the company's demise. While admitting that the actions were wrong, Lay minimized his role in them. He preserved his ethical image, at least in his own mind.

Ethical spinning is also inherent in the cliché "Everybody's doing it." We all cheat on our taxes, don't we? So powerful is this rationalization through blanket blame that it was Ben Johnson's defense for steroid use, which cost him his 1988 Olympic Gold Medal. This rationalization itself may be subject to bias. Ann has found that the more tempted we are to behave unethically, the more common—and thus acceptable—we perceive the unethical action to be.[16] That is, the bigger the deduction you'll get for cheating on your taxes, the more likely you will be to believe that others are cheating as well.

If you can't manage to spin your ethical behavior to your advantage, you can always change your ethical standards. In professions that require employees to bill their hours, such as consulting or the law, new employees may strongly believe they would never bill hours they hadn't accrued. As time goes on, however, an employee might once find herself short an hour of the "standard" billable hours. To make up this shortage, she adds fifteen minutes each to four projects. What's the big deal about rounding up? The big deal is what has happened psychologically. The ethical standard to which the employee held herself has shifted. The line between what is ethical and what is unethical has changed.

Once someone has adjusted her ethical standards, the power of her moral principles diminishes. There may no longer be a line she won't cross. This process occurs so gradually and incrementally that she won't discern each step she takes. A month after fudging her time by an hour, the consultant may find she has a two-hour deficit. Adding an additional hour for the week becomes the "new normal," and she doesn't even code it as being unethical anymore. Over time, the consultant may find herself overbilling by ten hours a week. Previously, she would never have found that amount of cheating to be acceptable under any circumstance, but the decision never involved ten hours of cheating; rather, she made a series of ten one-hour decisions—and a small adjustment to her ethical standard each time. To make matters worse, we can become desensitized as our exposure to unethical behavior increases. For the consultant, as ethical numbness sets in, each one-hour lie becomes less ethically painful. And to take a more dramatic example, prison counselors on "execution support teams," who work with the families of inmates and their victims, tend to become more and more morally disengaged the more executions they witness.[17]

Accounts of Bernard Madoff's Ponzi scheme suggest just how slippery a slope can become. Madoff's scheme involved paying certain investors with the money from other investors, a practice that allegedly began when Madoff lost money on trades and needed a little extra cash to cover the losses from those investments. Over time, the amount of cash Madoff needed to cover his losses grew—and so did the extent of his deception. So incremental was the scam that it went unnoticed by regulators for at least thirty years. Why didn't Madoff's auditors notice his transgressions? Having analyzed how our own unethical decisions come about, in the next chapter we will consider the related question of how we so often fail to fully notice and act on the unethical behavior of others.

Chapter 5

When We Ignore Unethical Behavior

Since the 2008 financial collapse, fingers have pointed in many directions. Targeted guilty parties have included irresponsible banks, greedy home-buyers, speculators, the Democratic Congress (for pushing to give low-income borrowers too much credit), and the Bush administration (for poor decision making and regulatory neglect). But at least part of the problem stems from the failure of independent credit-rating agencies to appropriately rate the riskiness of the mortgage-backed securities they assessed. "The story of the credit rating agencies is a story of colossal failure," according to Representative Henry Waxman (D-CA), chairman of the House Oversight and Government Reform Committee.[1] Waxman's committee found strong evidence that the executives in charge of the rating agencies were "well aware that there was little basis for giving AAA ratings to thousands of increasingly complex mortgage-related securities, but the companies often vouched for them anyway."

The purpose of credit-rating agencies is to educate outside stakeholders of the creditworthiness of issuers of debt obligations (including companies, nonprofit organizations, and federal, state, and local governments) as well as the debt instruments these financial organizations sell to the public. These agencies exist because of their presumed objectivity, yet their compensation has been tied to anything but objectivity. Former high-level employees of the rating agencies testified before Waxman's committee that a conflict of interest exists in the U.S. credit-rating system. Specifically, the largest credit-rating agencies—including Standard & Poor's, Moody's, and Fitch—are paid by the companies they rate in-

stead of by the investors who have the most to lose from inaccurate ratings. The largest ratings agencies have made enormous profits by giving
top ratings to securities and debt issuers, and not necessarily by providing
the most accurate assessments of these securities and issuers. In addition, agencies with the most lax standards have been, not surprisingly,
best at winning business from new clients, giving the agencies financial
incentives to positively assess securities. Compounding the problem further, the rating agencies have been selling consulting services to the same
firms whose securities they have been rating.

It may seem obvious that if rating agencies have an incentive to please
the companies they assess, an environment emerges in which independent, unbiased assessments are no longer possible. Yet not everyone believes this is an obvious conclusion. Defenders of the rating agencies have
argued that the agencies' knowledge of the importance of ensuring a
firm's integrity would protect them from issuing biased assessments. This
belief, while admirable, is overly optimistic. Worse yet, it prevented society
from seeing the unethical behavior of the parties involved. Just as the federal government failed to address the inherent conflict of interest in the
auditing industry in the pre-Enron era, our leaders failed to make changes
to the credit-rating industry that might have headed off disaster. In both
cases, the unethical behavior of others appeared opaque to many people.

There are many reasons why we do not notice the unethical behavior
of others. To begin with, we are busy paying attention to other things. As
we will discuss in more detail in chapter 6, we pay attention to goals for
which we receive rewards and too often ignore those for which we do not.
We are not usually rewarded for noticing the unethical behavior of others.
What's more, human beings have a remarkable ability to overlook the
obvious. In one study, psychologist Ulric Neisser asked his Cornell undergraduate students to watch a video in which two visually superimposed
groups of three players were passing basketballs.[2] One trio wore white
shirts, and the other trio wore dark shirts. The students in Neisser's study
were instructed to count the number of passes made among the trio
wearing white shirts. The dual video, as well as the grainy nature of the
film, made the task moderately complex. Before reading on, feel free to

watch the video and try to accurately count the passes among players wearing the white shirts at www.blindspots-ethics.com/neisser.

As you may have guessed, this is a trick experiment. While you were busy counting passes, you—like most people who try this task—probably failed to see a woman who clearly and unexpectedly walked through the basketball court carrying an open umbrella. (If you don't believe she was there, go look again.) Only one in five of Neisser's Cornell undergraduate participants spotted the woman with the umbrella. When we show this video in our classrooms to MBA and executive students, far fewer than one in five people notice the woman, just as we failed to notice her when we first watched the video. Because they are focusing closely on one task—in this case, counting passes—people miss very obvious information in their visual world.

Neisser's video offers evidence that our focus on one set of tasks can blind us to other readily available information in our environment. Moving beyond simple busyness and distraction as an answer, using the lens of behavioral ethics, this chapter maps the multiple reasons why we overlook the unethical behavior of others. Why do we look the other way when, objectively, it should be clear to us that someone is doing something wrong? We begin by discussing the role of motivated blindness, or the tendency for people to overlook the unethical behavior of others when it is not in their best interest to notice the infraction. Second, we explore indirect blindness, or the tendency not to notice unethical actions when people do their dirty work through the behavior of others. Third, we examine the role of a slippery slope in noticing the unethical behavior of others. Finally, we examine how the tendency to value outcomes over processes can affect people's assessments of the ethicality of others' choices.

Motivated Blindness

In the controversial 2008 fictional film *The Reader*, based on the novel of the same name by the German writer Bernhard Schlink, an illiterate former Nazi guard, Hanna Schmitz, faces charges in a war crimes trial for a terrible episode she took part in during World War II. Schmitz and five other female SS guards were leading hundreds of prisoners in a death march in 1944. One night, the prisoners camped in a church for shelter, and the guards locked them in. The church was bombed and caught fire, but none of the guards unlocked the doors, and the three hundred prisoners burned to death inside.

Not only did Hanna fail to save the three hundred prisoners, but she also testified that, during the war, she had followed orders and chosen ten prisoners to send to the gas chambers of Auschwitz each month. When asked during the trial about her failure to unlock the doors of the church, Hanna (played by actress Kate Winslet) gives the judge a confused look. "Obviously," she says matter-of-factly, "for the obvious reason: we couldn't. We were guards. Our job was to guard the prisoners."[3] If the guards had freed the prisoners from the burning church, Hanna explains, they would not have been able to control the crowd. In the chaos, the prisoners would have escaped, and Hanna would not have performed her job properly. Pressed further to explain why she failed to free the prisoners, Hanna shouts, "We were responsible for them!" Bewildered, she asks the judge, "What would you have done?"

We have no interest in defending the actions of this fictional character. But the portrayal of Hanna in *The Reader*, to the consternation of some Jewish groups that criticized the story, suggests that the character did terrible things without recognizing the ethical implications of her actions. She was uneducated, grew up following the orders of superiors, took a position with the SS for practical reasons, and simply did not see the option of freeing the prisoners trapped in the burning church. In *The Reader*, Hanna accepts her fate (prison), but throughout much of her life, she fails to view her own behavior as unethical.

Hanna's behavior—and her denial that she did anything wrong—is an extreme case, and it is a fictional case. However, we argue that Hanna's lack of recognition parallels what many do wrong in the interest of their group, organization, or country. This behavior is consistent with emerging evidence that significant numbers of people are capable of engaging in massive harm without realizing they are doing so. In a 2009 study of 2,800 employees, 49 percent reported they had observed some type of wrongdoing on the job in the previous year, despite the considerable efforts that organizations are taking to improve their employees' ethical behavior. Unfortunately, wrongdoing isn't a new fad: The ethical scandals at Arthur Andersen, Enron, Health-South, Tyco, and WorldCom were preceded by earlier ethical scandals at General Electric, Investors Overseas Services, Lincoln Savings & Loan, Sears, and Shoney's.

Throughout this book, we have noted a core finding of behavioral ethics: that people who have a vested self-interest in a situation have difficulty approaching the situation without bias, even when they view themselves as honest. Here we argue that this bias extends to the observation of others: that is, if you are motivated to turn a blind eye to someone's unethical behavior, you won't see it. The term *motivated blindness* describes the common failure of people to notice others' unethical behavior when seeing that behavior would harm the observer. When party A has an incentive to see party B in a favorable light, party A will have difficulty accurately assessing the ethicality of party B's behavior. Across most major scandals of the last decade, many people—members of boards of directors, auditing firms, rating agencies, and so on—had access to the appropriate data and should have noticed and acted on the unethical behavior of others. Yet they did not do so, at least in part because of the psychological tendency not to notice bad data that we would prefer not to see.

One striking aspect of the story of the credit-rating agencies is how closely it resembles the story of auditing firms that emerged about seven years earlier. The most prominent scandal in the early part of the new millennium was the fall of Enron, the most famous business collapse of our time. How did Arthur Andersen, Enron's auditor, vouch for the firm's financial health during the time that Enron was concealing billions of dollars in debt from its shareholders? Quite simply, Arthur Andersen had ample reason to be afflicted by motivated blindness. In 2001, Andersen earned millions from Enron, then its second-largest client: $25 million in auditing fees and $27 million in consulting fees. Andersen had a strong motivation to retain and build on these lucrative contracts. Obviously, finding problems with your auditing client's books is no way to keep it as an ongoing client. In addition, it is likely that many Andersen auditors hoped to be hired by Enron, as a number of their colleagues had been.

Enron's collapse was not unique. Soon after the company's fall, major financial scandals unfolded at other major corporations, including World-Com, Global Crossing, Tyco International, and Parmalat. In each case, auditors were implicated for failing to bring wrongdoing to light. These scandals may not have occurred if members of these firms had taken note of the unethical behavior of their colleagues and clients rather than over-looking it. These cases shed light on a weakness of the U.S. auditing sys-tem: it allows motivated blindness to thrive.

Max and his colleagues tested the strength of such conflicts of interest by giving study participants information about the potential sale of a fic-tional company. The participants' task was to estimate the company's value.[4] Participants were assigned to one of four roles: buyer, seller, buy-er's auditor, or seller's auditor. All participants read the same informa-tion, including information that could help them estimate the worth of the firm. Those acting as auditors provided estimated valuations of the company's worth to their clients. As the literature on self-serving biases discussed earlier in the book would suggest, sellers submitted higher es-timates of the company's worth than did prospective buyers.[5] More rele-vant to this chapter, the auditors, who were advising either the buyer or the seller, were strongly biased toward the interests of their clients: sell-ers' auditors publicly concluded that the firm was worth far more than did buyers' auditors.

Were the auditors' judgments intentionally biased, or was bounded ethicality at play? To answer this question, the auditors were asked to esti-mate the company's true value, as assessed by impartial experts, and were told they would be rewarded for the accuracy of their private judgments. Auditors for the sellers reached estimates of the company's value that, on average, were 30 percent higher than the estimates of auditors who served buyers. This evidence shows that, rather than making a conscious decision to favor their clients, the participants assimilated information about the target company in a biased way. Being in the role of the auditor biased their estimates and limited their ability to notice the bias in their clients' behavior. Thus, even a purely hypothetical relationship between an auditor and a client distorted the judgments of those playing the role of auditor. Furthermore, we replicated this study with actual auditors from one of the "Final Four" large auditing firms as our participants and received similar results. Undoubtedly, a long-standing relationship involving millions of dollars in ongoing revenues would have an even stronger effect.

When a client behaves unethically, its auditor doesn't see this unethical behavior for the same reason the client doesn't see its own unethical behavior. Bias in the direction of those who pay their bills (their clients) prevents auditors from distancing themselves from their clients. From the perspective of behavioral ethics, auditors become more like their clients than they would be if no such motivation existed; as a result, they are unlikely to see the unethical actions and biases in their clients' behavior. The client's bounded ethicality transfers to the auditor.

Motivated blindness appears to be responsible for the failure to notice others' unethical behavior in many domains. Consider the widespread use of steroids in baseball. In 2007, Barry Bonds of the San Francisco Giants surpassed Hank Aaron to become the all-time leader in career home runs, perhaps the most valued record in Major League Baseball. Law enforcement agencies, the baseball commissioner, and fans now question whether Bonds's performance truly surpassed that of Aaron. Many believe that Bonds used steroids or other drugs to improve his performance, especially given that his longtime trainer was indicted for supplying steroids to athletes. Similar suspicions have swirled around other MLB superstars, including Sammy Sosa, Roger Clemens, David Ortiz, Manny Ramirez, and others. In July 2009 it surfaced that MLB had known of at least 100 players who had tested positive for using performance-enhancing drugs.

In light of the steroid scandal, baseball fans tend to direct their wrath at the players who cheated (and got caught) for tainting the sport. Yet the nature of competition in Major League Baseball, the related financial rewards, and lax enforcement of drug rules were all contributing factors that gave players a strong incentive to use steroids. In fact, many players may have felt they would have been at an unfair disadvantage if they *didn't* use steroids. Fingers should also be pointed at the MLB commissioner, the San Francisco Giants team, and the players' union. None of these groups investigated the rapid changes in Bonds's and other players' physical appearances, their enhanced strength, and their increased power at the plate as these changes occurred. Given that sports journalists and many fans understood that a massive steroid problem existed throughout MLB, why didn't the commissioner, individual teams, or the players' union address the problem? The answer, we believe, lies in the fact that these groups benefited financially, at least in the short term, from the steroid use of players such as Bonds. Steroid use led to home runs, home runs increased attendance, and increased attendance generated more profit for the league, the teams, and the players. These benefits prevented MLB management from noticing problems it preferred not to see.

Was steroid use that easy to notice? Take a look for yourself. In figure 6 we plot the number of home runs hit by the players with the first-, second-, and third-most home runs each year from 1990 to 2009. The peaks between 1998 and 2001, typically recognized as the height of the steroid era in baseball, should have provided reasonably good evidence for the MLB to act (along with the other evidence available). To rule out the possibility that a few stellar players during this era skewed the results, we averaged the number of home runs hit by the home run leader from 1991 to 1994. This average was forty-four. We then counted the number of players in each year of the 1998–2001 steroid era who hit that number of home runs or more. Ten players in 1998, eight players in 1999, six players in 2000, and nine players in 2001 matched or beat the average number of home runs hit by the home run leaders between 1991 and 1994. This simple arithmetic suggests that an extraordinary number of players were hitting balls out of the park during the steroid era—and that noticing these unusual statistics shouldn't have been difficult.

Motivated blindness can cause people at the highest levels of society to engage in behaviors that they would never condone with greater aware-

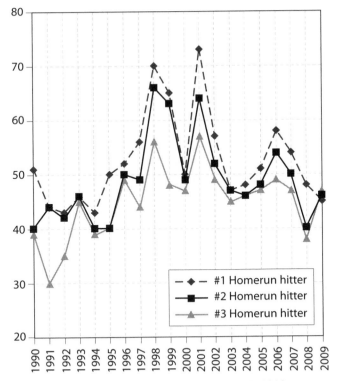

Figure 6. Home runs hit by the top three MLB players, 1990–2009

ness. Consider the child sexual abuse scandals that have rocked the Catholic Church. How did the abuse run rampant for decades without being stopped by the church's hierarchy? To take one striking example, Cardinal Bernard F. Law, the archbishop of Boston, failed to act on the enormous amount of child abuse that occurred under his jurisdiction. He admitted in court papers that he knew about accusations against John J. Geoghan, later convicted as a child molester, yet Law returned the priest to parish work. Law also admitted that he kept James Foley active in his ministry despite learning in 1993 that the priest had fathered two children with a woman in his parish and, in 1973, had fled the scene when she took a lethal dose of pills in an apparent suicide attempt. Law kept many other criminals and church rule-breakers active in the priesthood.[6]

Making the question more complex, Cardinal Law, a former civil rights activist, had dedicated his life to helping others. All the evidence suggests that Law was an ethical person who made some very highly unethical and probably illegal decisions in his executive role. Why did he tolerate illegal, abusive behavior? Law testified that, in retrospect, he relied on outdated medical and psychiatric advice regarding the ability of the abusers to curtail their behavior when deciding whether to keep them in the church. It is quite possible that Cardinal Law believed that priests such as Geoghan would be able to control their behavior. It is also possible that Cardinal Law's desire for abusers to be reformed blinded him to obvious evidence that the immoral and criminal behavior was likely to be repeated.

More recently, Cardinal Joseph Ratzinger, the current pope, has been accused of cover-ups of other sex abuse scandals within the Catholic Church, including last-minute transfers of accused priests to other parishes and emphasizing loyalty to the church over truly ethical responsible behavior. Without excusing any behavior that led to the abuse of children, we believe that it is possible that the pope's loyalty to his organization may have blinded him to the seriousness of his actions. Rather than a defense of unethical behavior, motivated blindness offers a psychological explanation of how unethical behavior may come about.

As shown in these examples and many others, we are not only blind to our own unethical actions but also to the unethicality of those around us. The motivation to remain blind to the unethical behavior of others comes at us in many forms, including fear, incentives, organizational loyalty, and organizational culture. To behave more ethically, we need to remove our blinders and examine the effects of these forces on our judgment.

Indirect Blindness

Imagine that your company produces a slow-selling item. It has few customers, but the ones who like the item would pay much more for it than you currently charge. Imagine that these customers are hostage to your pricing increases because you have a monopoly on the product and because they need it to stay healthy. You are aware that any significant increase in the product's price would attract negative publicity that would cost you more than you would gain from the price increase. What would you do to solve this puzzle?

In August 2005, Merck, a major pharmaceutical firm, found an answer. Merck sold off a slow-selling but effective cancer drug named Mustargen to Ovation, a smaller pharmaceutical firm, along with a second cancer drug called Cosmegen.[7] A chemotherapy drug used to treat lymphoma, Mustargen was used by fewer than 5,000 patients and generated annual sales of only about $1 million for Merck at the time it was sold.

At first glance, it looks as if Merck had found an effective means of moving a slow-moving drug out its busy manufacturing system. But it turns out that manufacturing Mustargen was not the issue for Merck. After selling the rights to Mustargen and Cosmegen to Ovation, Merck continued to manufacture the drugs for Ovation on a contract basis.

If making a small amount of a product was inefficient, why would Merck continue to produce Mustargen? Consider what happened after Merck completed its deal with Ovation: Ovation increased the price of Mustargen by approximately tenfold and raised the price of Cosmegen by even more. It turns out that Ovation often buys small-market drugs from visible pharmaceutical firms that have public-relations problems associated with dramatically increasing the price of drugs needed by their consumers. In a different transaction, Ovation purchased the drug Panhematin from Abbott Laboratories and increased the price nearly tenfold; Abbott continued to manufacture the drug. Merck's decision to sell Mustargen and Cosmegen to Ovation suggests that its leaders hoped to see headlines such as "Merck Sells Two Drugs to Ovation" rather than headlines such as "Merck Gouges Cancer Patients, Increases Cancer Drug Prices by 1,000 percent."

How did Merck get away with this clever strategy? Merck succeeded because human intuition does not sufficiently hold people and organizations accountable for such indirect unethical behavior. Even when data suggesting unethical intent is obvious, we still let those who behaved unethically off the hook. Notice that we are not commenting on the ethicality of increasing prices for needed cancer medication. In fact, we generally believe that high profits in the pharmaceutical sector have helped to create the vast array of amazing drugs that are available to patients today. But it is important to become aware of how difficult it is to "see" the indirect but unethical actions of others; this awareness can help us identify individuals and organizations that intentionally create opaqueness. If Merck did indeed assume that a tenfold price increase in a cancer drug would attract negative attention, we believe most people would view the decision to hide the increase through an intermediary such as Ovation as a manipulative, unethical strategy. Merck's apparent strategy often works, as do many other similar strategies, because the public and the press too often fail to notice the dirty work that individuals and organizations perform through intermediaries. Most of us fail to hold others sufficiently accountable for their indirect unethical actions.

This argument was tested more precisely by Max and his colleagues in an experimental study designed to mirror the environment of the Merck story.[8] Participants in the study read the following passage:

> A major pharmaceutical company, X, had a cancer drug that was minimally profitable. The fixed costs were high and the market was limited. But, the patients who used the drug really needed it. The pharmaceutical was making the drug for $2.50/pill (all costs included), and was only selling it for $3/pill.

The participants were then divided into two groups. Members of one of the groups were asked to assess the ethicality of the following action:

A. The major pharmaceutical firm raised the price of the drug from $3 per pill to $9 per pill.

The other group was asked to assess the ethicality of a different course of action:

B. The major pharmaceutical X sold the rights to a smaller pharmaceutical. In order to recoup costs, company Y increased the price of the drug to $15 per pill.

As we expected, people who read action A judged the behavior of the pharmaceutical firm more harshly than did participants who read action B, despite the fact that action A would have had a smaller financial impact on patients.

It is useful to note that these participants responded to only one of the two options, not to both (what experimental researchers call a "between-subjects design"). We then went on to present a third group of participants with both possible actions and asked them to judge which action was more unethical. Now the preferences were reversed: When they could compare the two scenarios, participants viewed action B as being more ethically problematic than action A. This finding is consistent with substantial research showing that this type of "side by side" or "joint" evaluation leads to more reflective and rational assessments than "separate" (one at a time) evaluations. Yet it is important to recognize that most real-world, morally questionable actions come to us one action at a time.

We replicated this result in domains other than drugs, such as contaminated land and pollution controls. We consistently found that when study participants were judging one option, they significantly discounted the unethicality of the focal firm acting through an intermediary. Yet when they were asked to compare an indirect action to a direct action, they saw through the indirectness and made their assessments based on the magnitude of the harm created by the action.[9] Further, we improved the transparency of the intent of the pharmaceutical firm in the indirect condition by making it clear that the firm understood the implications of selling off the drug and would profit by doing so. Even with extraordinary transparency, participants viewed indirect action, under separate evaluation, to be less unethical than direct action.

Finally, an economist, Luke Coffman, turned our question into an experimental game in which the goal was to find out how much other actors would punish a party for acting unethically either directly versus indirectly.[10] Luke created what he calls a "four-player dictator game." In the more common two-person dictator game, player A is given a fixed amount of money and faces a choice between giving none, some, or all of this money to player C. Player C is a passive recipient of player A's decision. In Luke's game, player A, who had $24, was given the option of playing the dictator game, as the dictator, with player C, or he could sell the rights to the game to player B at a negotiated price. If player B bought the game from player A, player B assumed the role of the dictator and had $24 to allocate in a dictator game played with player C. The final step in the game is that player D had the opportunity to punish player A (but not player B) for his actions by reducing player A's final payoff. As expected, when player A stayed in the game (i.e., did not sell the rights to the game to player B), player D typically punished player A for giving smaller amounts to player C, with the size of the punishment directly related to the amount of money player A kept for himself. More interestingly, and consistent with our studies, when player A did sell the rights to the game to player B, rather than choosing to be a greedy dictator, player D decreased the amount of punishment dramatically. That is, participants punished those who engaged in direct unethical behavior more than they punished those who engaged in indirect unethical behavior. This difference held up even when the net harm to player C was the same, and in later versions, when player A could fully predict how player B's decisions would affect player C.

This type of behavioral ethics research demonstrates that by engaging in indirect action under predictable circumstances, decision makers trigger *indirect blindness* in the eyes of observers and thus are let off the hook for the harms they cause. Members of organizations routinely delegate unethical behavior to others in their organizations. Managers tell their subordinates to "do whatever it takes" to achieve production or sales goals, for example, leaving open the possibility of aggressive or even unethical tactics. U.S. companies outsource production to offshore subcontractors that are inexpensive because they are less constrained by costly labor and environmental ethical standards. Partners at accounting firms remind junior auditors about the importance of retaining a client that has inappropriate accounting practices. Across many other situations, people overlook the problematic ethical implications of others' behavior when the actions occur indirectly.

Here's another example. Max lives in Boston, is a longtime football fan, and doesn't like cheaters. Thus, Max was quite disappointed by behavior that occurred during the 2007 National Football League's season. The New England Patriots in that year were arguably one of the greatest football teams of all time. Unfortunately, Bill Belichick, the team's highly visible head coach, threatened the team's reputation by blatantly cheating. When the Patriots were playing the New York Jets (a weak team) early in the 2007 season, Belichick directed an assistant to film the Jets' private defensive signals—a clear violation of the rules, as Belichick well knew.[11] NFL commissioner Roger Goodell fined Belichick $500,000, fined the Patriots $250,000, and penalized the Patriots in the form of taking away one of their future high-value draft choices.

Clearly, Belichick was guilty. But what about the Kraft family, which owns the Patriots? They hired Belichick, encouraged him to win, and offered no criticism of the coach after the incident. The ethics of the Kraft family were largely unquestioned by the media, and Patriots fans did not seem overly concerned about the reputable family's behavior. The Kraft family's notable silence on the issue was indirectly unethical and, as a result, went unnoticed.

When people stand by the unethical actions of their subordinates, they own that unethical action. Their silence suggests that their only problem with the unethical action is that it was detected. We should hold executives accountable for the actions of their employees when all evidence suggests that the organization tolerated unethical behavior. Unfortunately, behavioral ethics research has provided abundant evidence that outsiders overlook the unethical actions of actors who work through indirect parties.

Unethical Behavior on a Slippery Slope

According to an interesting folk tale, if you place a frog in a pot of hot water, the frog will jump out. However, if you put the frog in a pot of warm water and raise the temperature gradually, the frog will not react to the gradual change in temperature, and it will cook to death. While the story happens to be untrue, it is a fine analogy for the failure of most people to notice the gradual erosion of ethical standards. As we suggested in the previous chapter, our unethical behavior often occurs on a slippery slope. We excuse ourselves for committing one tiny infraction and then allow ourselves to commit increasingly unethical infractions as time passes.

Behavioral ethics research shows that people also commonly fail to notice the slippery slope of *others'* unethical behavior. In addition to Bernard Madoff's feeder funds, the broader professional investment community and the U.S. Securities and Exchange Commission (SEC) did not notice that his funds' performance was inconceivable. Why not? Part of the story is motivated blindness. Another part, though, is that this fraud developed slowly, over at least a fifteen-year period. When fraud occurs on a slippery slope, the impossibility of returns such as Madoff's is likely to go unnoticed.

In fact, people are capable of ignoring clear warning signals of others' unethical behavior. Beginning in 1999, independent financial fraud investigator Harry Markopolos repeatedly attempted to warn the SEC that Madoff's returns were not legally possible. Yet all indications suggest that the SEC did not take these accurate warnings seriously. As a result, Madoff's fraud involving more than $50 billion didn't come to light until the mega-swindler himself confessed.

Now imagine that an accountant with a large auditing firm (perhaps Arthur Andersen) is in charge of the audit of a large company (perhaps Enron) with a strong reputation. For three years in a row, the client's financial statements are extremely ethical and of high quality. As a result, the auditor approves the statements and has an excellent relationship with its client. The next year, however, the company commits clear transgressions in its financial statements, stretching and even breaking the law in certain areas.

Now imagine a different scenario. This time, the auditor notices that the corporation stretches the law in a few areas the first year but does not appear to break the law. The next year, the firm is even more unethical, committing a minor violation of federal accounting standards. The third year, the violations are a bit more severe. In the fourth year, the auditing firm finds itself facing the type of severe violations described in the previous paragraph, in which the client crosses the ethical line abruptly.

How is the corporation's auditor likely to react in each of these two scenarios? In the first situation, the auditor probably would refuse to certify that the financial statements were acceptable according to government regulations. In the second scenario, it is far less likely that the auditor would notice the same severe ethical transgression. In other words, auditors would be more likely to notice and refuse to sign the statements in the first version of the story than in the second one, even if the unethical behavior was the same in the last year described in both stories.[12]

In our research with David Messick and Francesca Gino, we explored whether this "slippery slope" pattern of behavior can explain the common failure to notice the egregious behavior of others.[13] Using laboratory studies with features similar to those described in these two stories, we found that people are less likely to perceive changes in others' unethical behavior if the changes occur slowly over time rather than abruptly.[14]

Visual perception research, such as the basketball-passing video that we described at the start of the chapter, demonstrates that we frequently fail to notice changes that occur right in front of our eyes.[15] In one study investigating "change blindness," an experimenter holding a basketball stopped pedestrians to ask for directions. As each pedestrian gave directions, a group of confederates (research assistants) walked between the experimenter and the pedestrian. As the confederates walked by, the experimenter handed the basketball to one of the confederates. After the pedestrian completed giving directions, the experimenter asked her if she had noticed any sort of change while she was talking. Most of the individuals in the study did not notice any change. Yet when they were asked directly if they had seen a basketball, many recalled seeing the basketball, and many could even recount specific characteristics of the ball. Thus, while the pedestrians failed to notice explicitly that a small, incremental (but obvious) change took place, it was possible that they could have done so had they been attuned to it. Similarly, many Madoff investors can now recount the evidence that they should have perceived long before he confessed to his crimes.

The scientific study of change blindness focuses on visual perception. People also fail to notice other types of changes in their environment that lead to significant decision-making errors with ethically relevant consequences. As a result, people are less likely to notice others' unethical behavior when it occurs in small increments—on a slippery slope—than when it occurs suddenly, a phenomenon that should put us on alert to slowly degrading ethical behavior.

Valuing Outcomes over Processes

Consider story A:

> A pharmaceutical researcher defines a clear protocol for determining whether or not to include clinical patients as data points in a study. He is running short of time to collect sufficient data points for his study within an important budgetary cycle in his firm. As the deadline approaches, he notices that four subjects were withdrawn from the analysis because of technicalities. He believes that the data derived from those four subjects in fact are appropriate to use, and when he adds those data points, the results move from not quite statistically significant to significant. He adds these data points, and soon the drug goes to market. This drug is later withdrawn from the market after it kills six patients and injures hundreds of others. How unethical do you view the researcher to be?

Now consider a somewhat different story, B:

> A pharmaceutical researcher defines a clear protocol for determining whether or not to include clinical patients as data points in a study. He is running short of time to collect sufficient data points for his study within an important budgetary cycle in his firm. He believes

that the product is safe and effective. As the deadline approaches, he notices that if he had four more data points for how subjects are likely to behave, the analysis would be significant. He makes up these data points, and soon the drug goes to market. This drug is a profitable and effective drug, and years later shows no significant side effects.

How unethical do you view this researcher in this second story to be? Which story do you find to be more egregious?

While we have shown you both stories, in a study based on them, we presented one story to one group of participants and the other story to another group of participants, such that each group only saw one story.[16] Those who read story A were more critical of the researcher in the story than were those who read story B. Those who read story A also reported that the behavior in the first story should be punished more harshly. Yet, as you probably noticed, the researcher's behavior was more unethical in story B than in story A.

Why would people view the behavior in story A as more egregious than the behavior in story B? The outcome bias provides an answer.[17] The outcome bias describes the tendency to take results into account, in a manner that is not logically justified, when evaluating the quality of the decision process that a decision maker used. Decision researchers Jon Baron and Jack Hershey were the first to find that in contexts ranging from simple laboratory gambles to medical decision-making, people judge the wisdom of decision makers based on the outcomes they obtain.

Our own research in behavioral ethics finds that people too often judge the ethicality of actions based on whether harm follows, rather than on the ethicality of the choice itself.[18] As in the research on direct versus indirect effects described earlier, people are affected by this bias when they confront one story or instance at a time. Clearly, the ability to see two versions of a story that have transparent differences allows us to avoid the outcome bias and to pay attention to and compare the actions of the two researchers. When this is done experimentally, people rate story B as more egregious than story A. But, as noted earlier, most of the time, the world presents us with one situation to assess at a time. Philosophers have long debated whether we should judge ethical actions based on the rules used to decide which action should be taken or based on the outcome itself. We expect this age-old debate will continue to be fiercely argued. However, when we judge an action based on its outcome and don't consider alternative options or scenarios (as is often the case), this judgment does not reflect the actor's underlying intentions.

The outcome bias is solidly integrated into our laws. Consider the story, told by psychologist Fiery Cushman and his colleagues, of two brothers, Jon and Mark, both of whom lack a criminal record or good marksmanship but possess a quick temper.[19] Imagine that a man confronts the two brothers and insults their family. Vowing to kill the guy, Jon pulls out a gun, but he misses his shot, and his target remains unharmed. By contrast, Matt decides he only wants to scare the man. He pulls out a gun, accidentally shoots the guy in the heart, and kills him. Cushman and colleagues note that in most U.S. states, Matt can expect a far longer prison sentence than Jon. In other words, the law pays more attention to outcomes than to intentions.

Cushman and colleagues have offered a brilliant experiment related to this hypothetical legal story and to the outcome bias. Simplifying the essence of their experiment, imagine that you face a choice between the following two options. You will be playing the game you choose with an unknown other person, also a participant in the experiment.

Option A: You roll a six-sided die. If it comes up a one, two, three, or four, you get $10 and the other party gets $0. If it comes up a five, you get $5 and the other party gets $5. If it comes up a six, you get $0, and the other party gets $10.

Option B: You roll a six-sided die. If it comes up a one, you get $10 and the other party gets $0. If it comes up a two, three, four, or five, you get $5 and the other party gets $5. If it comes up a six, you get $0 and the other party gets $10.

Notice that option A is the greedy choice, as it offers you more opportunities (four out of six, to be exact) to claim $10 for yourself. By contrast, option B is the fair choice, at least most of the time, as it offers four opportunities for the $10 to be split evenly between you and the other party. Regardless of which choice you make, any of the three outcomes described is possible; it's just their probabilities that differ.

After you choose which game to play, the die is rolled and the money is paid. Cushman and colleagues then allow the other party to punish you, the chooser, by reducing your payment without incurring any cost herself. The fascinating result is that when allocating punishment, the other party typically pays more attention to the equality of the result of the rolled die—a random outcome—than to the chooser's sense of fairness (as demonstrated by which option she chose). For example, if you chose to be fair and play option B, and then rolled a one, the other party is more likely to punish you than she would if you had greedily chosen option A and rolled a five.

These results clarify our unfortunate tendency to blame people too harshly for making sensible decisions that have unlucky outcomes. Compounding the problem, judging decisions based on their outcomes means that we often wait too long to condemn unethical behavior—until after a bad outcome has occurred. Many people now question the ethics of the Bush administration's decision to invade Iraq in 2003, including its misrepresentation of the "facts" that prompted the war. But criticism of the invasion was limited in much of the United States when it seemed as if the war was going well. When the war began to drag on, many more people began to question the Bush administration's prewar tactics, such as unfounded claims of evidence of weapons of mass destruction in Iraq. The outcome bias may partially explain why so many reserved judgment on the decision to go to war until they knew what the outcome would be. We often fail to take notice of unethical behavior—and condemn it only after a harmful outcome occurs.

We now return to the case of auditors at another level of analysis. For decades, U.S. auditing firms provided both auditing and consulting services to their clients. As we noted earlier, this situation logically and psychologically compromised the independence of their audits.[20] Long before Enron's collapse, we had ample evidence that the existing structure compromised the ethics of the auditing profession.[21] Despite added evidence of the failure of auditor independence and the widespread belief that independence was essential for reliable audits, it took the glaringly obvious failures of Enron, WorldCom, Tyco, and other firms to persuade the U.S. government to address the underlying conflicts of interest that compromised auditors.[22] Only these very bad outcomes motivated our legislative representatives to address the problem. But, for reasons that we will explore in chapter 7, even these changes were insufficient and poorly crafted to solve the core problem.

The outcome bias is related to research on identifiable victims.[23] The "identifiable victim effect" refers to the finding that people tend to be far more concerned with and show more sympathy for identifiable victims than statistical victims. Identifiable victims are specific people, while statistical victims are unknown, unspecified people. People tend to feel more concern for specific victims, even when no useful personalizing information about the victim is available (e.g., only a name is provided).[24] Now consider that the same unethical action could harm an identifiable victim, an unidentifiable victim, or no victim at all. Just as we often fail to notice unethical behavior when no victims have yet been affected by it, we are less likely to see the presence of unethical behavior when statistical victims are affected than when the victims are identifiable. Once again, differences in judgments of ethical behavior depend on the outcome of the unethical action, including our perceptions of who was affected, even though the perpetrator's actions remain the same.

The story of Noreen Harrington, a Goldman Sachs veteran who was the whistleblower in the mutual fund late-trading scandal, illustrates how depersonalizing the victims of our unethical behavior allows such behavior to be perpetuated.[25] The scandals involved two questionable practices: late trading, or the illegal practice of buying and selling funds after the 4:00 P.M. market close but still receiving the 4:00 P.M. price; and market timing, which involves exploiting prices via time zone differences in international funds, a practice that is legal but can be in violation of fund rules, as it often profits "market timers" at the expense of long-term shareholders. Harrington has said that prior to blowing the whistle on

these practices, she viewed them as part of "a nameless, faceless business
. . . in this business this is how you look at it. You don't look at it with a
face."[26] That view changed, she said, when her older sister asked her for
advice on her 401(k) account. Her sister, whom Harrington characterized
as one of the hardest workers she knew, was worried that the losses she
saw in her retirement account would prevent her from retiring. Suddenly,
Harrington "thought about this from a different vantage point," she explains. "I saw one face—my sister's face—and then I saw the faces of everyone whose only asset was a 401(k). At that point I felt the need to try
and make the regulators look into [these] abuses."[27]

Our own industry—higher education—is not immune from this bias.
In our discussion of in-group favoritism in chapter 3, we discussed the
widespread policy of universities admitting the underqualified children
of alumni. To our surprise, few commentators have publicly objected to
the policy of admitting such underperforming "legacies." The lack of out-
rage over this ethically questionable practice is likely due in part to the
difficulty of identifying the victims of such practices—that is, those who
are denied admission. Because the victims of legacy admissions policies
are statistical rather than identifiable, people fail to perceive that these
practices cause harm, and the behavior of those responsible goes unchecked. Even when we do recognize the negative outcome of such policies in theory, we are often dulled by their lack of vividness when we do
not know who was actually harmed.

Behavioral ethics research supports the argument that most people
want to act ethically. Yet we still find ourselves engaging in unethical behavior because of biases that influence our decisions—biases of which we
may not be fully aware. As we have noted in this chapter, these biases affect not only our own behavior, but also our ability to see the unethical
behavior of others. Having completed our overview of the systematic mistakes the human mind makes in ethical domains, in the next three chapters, we will use this knowledge to explore implications for organizations
and society, as well as opportunities to change these dysfunctional patterns of behavior.

Chapter 6

Placing False Hope in the "Ethical Organization"

In 2009, a group of thirty-three second-year MBA students at Harvard Business School wrote an oath that they asked their fellow students at Harvard to sign. The signatories vowed that, upon entering the workforce as managers, they would serve the greater good, act ethically, and refrain from self-interested acts within their organizations (see the oath at right). Within weeks, more than half of Harvard's 2009 MBA class had signed the oath. Soon it went viral, attracting signatures from large numbers of students and graduates of different MBA programs around the world. Some view the oath as a promising sign that new MBAs were rejecting the scandals of the recent past, such as the Bernard Madoff and AIG bonuses, and signaling a new era of corporate social responsibility.

While the attention that the oath brought to the issue of business ethics is valuable, the oath has attracted criticism as well. "There's no cost," Scott Holley, a 2009 Harvard MBA graduate and oath signer, told *Business-Week*. "You say the oath, and you're done."[1] Not only did Holley believe the oath would have little impact on managers' behavior, he thought it could become a symbol of hypocrisy if any of the signatories was later involved in an ethical scandal. Holley speculated that those most likely to sign the oath were those who had no intention of complying with it. Other critics have noted that the broad scope of the oath creates a potential clash of goals—such as balancing shareholder interests with the desire to protect the natural environment—that would be difficult to resolve. And some have commented that the oath could be moot if organizational leaders make unethical decisions that undermine the good intentions of individual managers.

THE MBA OATH

As a manager, my purpose is to serve the greater good by bringing people and resources together to create value that no single individual can create alone. Therefore I will seek a course that enhances the value my enterprise can create for society over the long term. I recognize my decisions can have far-reaching consequences that affect the well-being of individuals inside and outside my enterprise, today and in the future. As I reconcile the interests of different constituencies, I will face choices that are not easy for me and others.

Therefore I promise:

- **I will** act with utmost integrity and pursue my work in an ethical manner.
- **I will** safeguard the interests of my shareholders, co-workers, customers and the society in which we operate.
- **I will** manage my enterprise in good faith, guarding against decisions and behavior that advance my own narrow ambitions but harm the enterprise and the societies it serves.
- **I will** understand and uphold, both in letter and in spirit, the laws and contracts governing my own conduct and that of my enterprise.
- **I will** take responsibility for my actions, and I will represent the performance and risks of my enterprise accurately and honestly.
- **I will** develop both myself and other managers under my supervision so that the profession continues to grow and contribute to the well-being of society.
- **I will** strive to create sustainable economic, social, and environmental prosperity worldwide.
- **I will** be accountable to my peers and they will be accountable to me for living by this oath.

This oath I make freely, and upon my honor.[2]

Potentially countering these negative perceptions is the fact that companies and institutions are already spending a great deal of time and money
to improve their ethicality. Ethics programs, which include initiatives
such as instating codes of ethics, ombudsmen, and ethics training, are
designed to convey the values of an organization and the ethical standards
the organization expects its employees to meet. In addition, compliance
programs, an increasingly important element of ethics programs, are
being designed to ensure that organizations meet governmental regulations in the ethics domain. In response to the ethics scandals of the 1990s,
for instance, the Sarbanes-Oxley Act of 2002 requires all 9,000 publicly
held corporations in the United States to employ "in-house watchdogs," or
compliance officers—a position almost unheard of prior to 2002. At Sun
Microsystems, the chief compliance officer holds ethics "boot camps" for
employees, focusing on business ethics and compliance with Sarbanes-
Oxley.[3] The company has developed and translated its online courses on
federal compliance into at least nine languages. All 32,000 Sun employees
are required to take the course, making it the first required training course
in the company's history.

The use of compliance initiatives to improve organizational ethics
isn't limited to companies that trade on Wall Street. In university athlet-
ics, "Compliance officers have become an athletic department's most important employee," writes the *New York Times*.[4] In a world where violations of intercollegiate rules and regulations can wreak havoc on coaches,
players, and the university's reputation, ensuring that everyone plays "by
the books" is increasingly viewed as a critical mission.

These initiatives don't come cheap. A recent survey of 217 large firms
indicated that for every billion dollars in revenue earned, the average
company spends one million dollars on compliance initiatives.[5] At Sun
Microsystems, the costs of compliance initiatives, including the time employees spend in compliance training courses, accountant and auditor
fees, and costs borne by the controller's office, are estimated to exceed $6
million annually. If these efforts worked, many might argue that these
dollars—just a drop in the bucket for many companies—are well spent.
But that's a big if. As we have highlighted, despite all of the time and

money that has been spent on these efforts and all of the laws and regulations that have been enacted, unethical behavior appears to be on the rise.

These results, while disappointing, were predictable. Even the most well-intentioned oaths and ethics programs will fail if the concept of bounded ethicality is not taken into account. One problem with ethics programs is that they assume employees are aware of the rules and know what they need to do to comply with them. As noted in chapters 3 and 4, however, bounded ethicality and ethical fading may obscure whether ethical behavior, and compliance, is even relevant in a given situation.

Oaths, compliance systems, and other organizational attempts at encouraging ethical behavior are not only failing to meet their goal of curbing unethical behavior in most cases, but can actually *promote* unethical behavior. Why? Because the architects of such systems often neglect to consider how the structure of these programs inadvertently influences unethical behavior. Consider that ethics programs are usually predicated on formal systems that hand out rewards for ethical behavior and punishment for unethical behavior. Such efforts are doomed because of the way individuals respond to these rewards and punishments. Moreover, even if we could design a program that took these behavioral responses into account, it still wouldn't be sufficient. Formal ethics and compliance programs represent only the tip of an organization's "ethical infrastructure."[6] Underlying formal systems are informal norms and pressures that exert far more influence on employee behavior than any formal efforts could. In addition to exploring how individuals react to the incentives of compliance systems, behavioral ethics digs deep into organizations: past their formal ethics programs and into the informal systems that teach employees what behavior is *really* expected of them.

Reward Systems Gone Awry

To understand the flaws built into most organizational ethics programs, consider the case of a parent who is trying to encourage his child to make her bed in the morning. The parent gives the child a star each time she makes the bed, and she can later cash in her stars in exchange for valued toy purchases. The parent is proud of this system, and it seems to work. Each day, the child makes her bed. Soon, however, the parent notices that the child, who used to be in charge of emptying the wastebaskets, is no longer doing so consistently. Upon further investigation, the parent learns that the child doesn't actually make her bed; she simply flattens the comforter on top of her unmade bed.

Like a reward system for chores, the goals of formal ethics programs—to decrease unethical behavior and increase ethical behavior—are commendable and, most likely, have few opponents. The reward systems that are built into these formal programs are based on the underlying premise of goal-setting research: Individuals seek information about behaviors that will be rewarded and then strive to perform well on those behaviors. Yet the downside to goal setting has been ignored, with perilous results. In fact, goals can create systematic problems. Specifically, they can encourage employees to

1. focus too narrowly on their goals, to the neglect of nongoal areas;
2. engage in risky behavior;
3. focus on extrinsic motivators and lose their intrinsic motivation;
4. and, most importantly from our perspective, engage in more unethical behavior than they would otherwise.[7]

Consider the recent financial crisis and its link to faulty reward systems. President Bill Clinton's objective of increasing homeownership by rewarding potential home buyers and lenders is one example. The Clinton administration "went to ridiculous lengths" to increase homeownership in the United States, promoting "paper-thin down payments" and pushing lenders to give mortgage loans to unqualified buyers, according to *BusinessWeek* editor Peter Coy. "It's clear now that the erosion of lending standards pushed prices up by increasing demand," writes Coy, "and later led to waves of defaults by people who never should have bought a home in the first place."[8]

Increasing the percentage of Americans who own a home arguably could be a commendable goal, one that, if accomplished, could result in a more just and ethical society. But Clinton and others who promoted this goal overlooked the way in which such goals change behavior, often in ways that are unintended and undesirable. In this case, the goal of increasing home ownership inadvertently spurred unethical lending by banks and risky decision making by consumers. Artificially imposed rewards, including low interest rates and down payments, were at the center of the epidemic of poor decision making.

To take a more historical example of a governmental initiative to promote ethical behavior and expose unethical behavior, the False Claims Act was passed in 1863 to address fraud by Union Army defense contractors during the Civil War. The act allows individuals and organizations who are unaffiliated with the U.S. government to file a claim against individuals and federal contractors that they believe have directly or indirectly defrauded the government. The goal of the act is to encourage citizens to become whistleblowers by exposing unethical behavior of which the government may be unaware. After a whistleblower files a lawsuit documenting alleged offenses in a U.S. district court, the Department of Justice conducts an investigation and decides whether to pursue the case. The *qui tam* provision of the act stipulates that whistleblowers who expose such cases will be rewarded a percentage of the money that the government recovers, with rewards as high as 30 percent of the recovery amount. Those rewards can be quite substantial: A recent settlement, based on TRW's efforts to prevent a scientist from revealing information about faulty electronic components the company sold to the government, was settled for $325 million; $48.8 million of this amount was awarded to the whistleblower and his attorneys.[9]

Clearly, the False Claims Act is well intentioned. It was designed to give citizens a strong incentive to take the personal and professional risks involved in reporting fraud. However, basing rewards on total damages could actually encourage prospective whistleblowers to delay reporting a known fraud, and even to actively participate in its continuance, in order to run up the total amount of damages incurred by the government and thus their percentage of the take.[10] Because of the potential corruption created by this faulty reward system, the reporting of wrongdoing can actually *increase* unethical behavior.

Organizational and governmental leaders have a responsibility to analyze how employees and citizens are likely to respond to proposed incentive systems. But as these examples demonstrate, the architects of reward systems often fail to consider how efforts to accomplish a target goal will cause decision makers to ignore ethical problems in other areas. Reward systems can promote a "whatever it takes" attitude that can be a powerful catalyst for unethical behavior. Such systems can be so effective in directing attention to the "ends"—the potential rewards of compliance and cooperation—that people overlook the means by which they will achieve the goal. As we argued in chapter 5, the competition and reward systems in Major League Baseball encouraged players and management to meet the goal of winning at any cost, a focus that resulted in a failure to see players' widespread abuse of steroids. For many years, players, who had a narrow window of time in which to cash in on their skills, faced little to no penalties for using steroids.

Corporations affect ethics in numerous ways, many of which have little explicit connection to ethics—until the unethical actions occur and become public. Consider what happened in the early 1990s when Sears gave its automotive mechanics a sales goal of $147 an hour. To meet this goal, employees overcharged for their services companywide and sold unnecessary repairs to customers. After the scandal was exposed, the company's chairman, Edward Brennan, admitted that the "goal setting process for service advisers created an environment where mistakes did occur."[11] The focus on racking up billable hours in accounting, consulting, and law firms creates similarly perverse incentives. Employees end up engaging in unnecessary and expensive projects to meet their often-unrealistic billable hour goals.

Psychologists Barry Staw and Richard Boettger have provided a powerful demonstration of what happens when individuals are told to focus narrowly on achieving a single goal.[12] They asked college students to proofread a paragraph that they were told would be used in a brochure promoting the university's business school. Grammatical and content errors were embedded within the paragraph. Some of the students were told to simply "do your best" when correcting the paragraph. Others were told to focus on correcting grammar mistakes. The researchers found that students who were instructed to "do your best" were more successful at finding both grammatical and content errors than those who were told to focus on correcting grammar mistakes. A narrow goal—namely, the instruction to find grammatical errors—led individuals to overlook obvious content errors.

In the U.S. health-care system, the focus of for-profit insurance companies on a primary goal—profits—has led to ethical lapses when it comes to meeting other goals, such as health-care delivery. In the midst of his 2009 push for health-care reform, President Obama delivered a speech to Congress in which he accused insurance companies of cherry-picking healthy clients and dropping sick ones. He cited the case of Robin Beaton, a Texas woman whose insurance company canceled her scheduled surgery for advanced-stage breast cancer because she forgot to disclose that she had recently been treated by a dermatologist for acne. According to Obama, the insurance companies make such unethical decisions because they are rewarded for doing so. "They do it because it's profitable," Obama said. "As one former insurance executive testified before Congress, insurance companies are not only encouraged to find reasons to drop the seriously ill; they are rewarded for it. All of this is in service of meeting what this former executive called 'Wall Street's relentless profit expectations.'"[13]

We don't find fault with the notion that insurance companies and other businesses should earn profits; in fact, we believe they should. Rather, we blame the reward systems that, by putting the goal of high profits above all others, leave ethical considerations in the dust.

One reason one-dimensional goals fail is because they cause individuals to be driven by an extrinsic motivation to comply rather than by an

intrinsic motivation to do what's right. Let's return to the problem of accurate reporting of billable hours in the legal, accounting, and consulting
fields. Some U.S. law firms have taken steps to increase the transparency
of billable hours in an effort to encourage employees to be more honest
about where and how they spend their time. This admirable goal trans-
lates into requirements for more detailed reporting of one's time. In some
cases, these requirements have generated literally hundreds of codes for
specific activities that a legal professional might undertake for a client.
One would think that such fine-grained accountability would increase the
honesty of reporting, but that's not necessarily the case. Lawyers have told
us that such detailed accounting has the reverse effect. Trying to decide
whether a specific research activity falls under category "x.1.2" or "z.2.4"
involves some guesswork, they tell us—guesswork that soon becomes a
natural component of the billable hour. Small guesses becomes large
guesses, and a system designed to promote ethical behavior backfires.[14]

Even when employees do consider multiple goals, the unbalanced attention they give to a primary goal tends to overshadow goals that are less
rewarded and therefore viewed as less important. Profit concerns tend to
dwarf sustainability efforts; similarly, the goal of on-time delivery can
cause firms to sacrifice quality. The case of corporate quarterly earnings is
another telling example. Research shows that, in comparison to firms
that issue longer-term earnings reports, firms that issue quarterly reports
accomplish their primary goal of meeting or beating analyst expectations.
However, these firms also devote fewer resources to the less publicized,
less rewarded (in the short term) goal of investing in research and development.[15] By focusing on meeting quarterly earnings goals, firms become
distracted from other important goals, such as investing in their long-
term viability. Moreover, many firms manipulate data to reach their quarterly goals or earning expectations, sacrificing long-term performance in
the process. General Electric, for example, was fined $50 million by the
SEC for pretending it had sold 100 locomotives that were actually sitting
idle, a move many analysts believed was driven by the desire to meet or
beat earnings expectations.[16]

Reward systems are usually well intentioned, yet they tend to miss the mark because they fail to anticipate how employees will respond to them. They are simplistic, focusing on a single objective. By ignoring how employees will achieve outlined goals, they produce unintentional behavior, and they discourage desirable behaviors that aren't rewarded. Like the child who is rewarded for making her bed, employees fail to take out the trash.

How can organizations design more ethical incentive systems? Most obviously, when setting goals for their members, they must try to take the perspective of those whose behavior they are trying to influence and think through their likely responses. Wall Street analysts and others who are responsible for evaluating firms' health need to think through the consequences of heavily weighting short-term earnings. By anticipating the potentially adverse behavior their reports and statements could promote, decision makers may find they have overlooked goals that are just as important to reward, if not more important, such as honest reporting. Given that the provision of accurate valuations is arguably our financial system's most important goal, leaders need to modify the system to include multiple, attainable objectives and appropriate checks and balances. When they fail to meet this responsibility, they can be viewed not only as promoting unethical behavior, but as engaging in it themselves.

The Unintended Effects of Sanctions

In addition to encouraging ethical behavior through rewards, ethics and compliance programs often include sanctioning systems that attempt to discourage *unethical* behavior, typically through punishment. Yet these programs often have the reverse effect, *encouraging* the very unethical behavior they are supposed to discourage.

In a set of experiments, Ann and her colleague David Messick found that the implementation of a compliance system can actually increase the undesirable behaviors the system was designed to decrease.[17] In one study, individuals played the role of a manufacturer in an industry that emits toxic gases. The participants were told that they and the other manufacturers in their industry were concerned that environmental groups would soon target them for emitting pollutants and that such attention would result in costly legislation and expensive "clean" solutions. Participants learned that, to avoid scrutiny from environmental groups, the manufacturers in their industry had met as a group and reached an agreement to run their "scrubbers" 80 percent of the time to clean up some of their emissions. The manufacturers saw this solution as a way to appease the environmentalists. Although running scrubbers is expensive, the manufacturers realized this strategy was less expensive than the legislation and compliance costs that would result if the environmental groups took the industry to task.

Each participant, playing the part of a manufacturer, was presented with the decision of whether to keep her company's promise and run the scrubbers or to renege on the promise and not run the scrubbers. Imagine that you are in the position of manufacturer X, who knew that his decision regarding whether or not to run the scrubbers would have no impact on whether the environmentalists came after the industry. Why? Because if every other manufacturer kept the promise and ran their scrubbers, then the total emissions level would fall below the radar. The environmentalists would leave the industry alone, whether or not manufacturer X ran its scrubbers. If, on the other hand, every other manufacturer abandoned the promise, then the continued high emissions levels would attract the attention of the environmentalists, and nothing manufacturer X could do would change that. So, independent of what the other manufacturers decided, manufacturer X knew that his least expensive option would be to renege on his promise and not run his scrubbers.

We told half of our participants that there would be no compliance system—in other words, that none of the manufacturers would be monitored or sanctioned to determine whether or not they were adhering to their promise. The other half were told that a compliance system would be in place, such that a small percentage (5 percent) of the manufacturers would be subject to random monitoring to check whether or not they were adhering to the agreement; if they were found to be in violation, they would be sanctioned and subject to a minimal fine.

Did their participants cooperate with the group, or did they behave unethically? As it turned out, whether or not they reneged depended on the presence or absence of a compliance system. Economists would predict that the presence of a possible fine should cause one of two things to occur: (1) there would be zero change in behavior (that is, manufacturers would not run their scrubbers) because the fine was so negligible that it would have no impact, or (2) because the fine made reneging less attractive, there would be greater adherence and more scrubbers running. In Ann and David's study, something very different occurred. Although the presence of a fine made reneging less attractive from a financial perspective, it actually led to *more* reneging, not less. When there was no compliance system, more than half of participants stuck by the promise and agreed to run their scrubbers. In the presence of a compliance system, however, less than half of participants stuck to the agreement; a majority reneged on the original commitment.

Ann and David traced their results to the lens through which the participants viewed the decision. When no compliance system was in place, most saw the decision as an ethical one. In this case, individuals appeared to be searching for an answer to the question, "What is the right thing to do?" By contrast, when a compliance system was in place, most participants believed they were making a business decision. In this case, they appeared to ask themselves this question instead: "What is the likelihood I will get caught, and how much will it cost me?" The imposition of a compliance system led to ethical fading, such that participants were less likely to see the decision as an ethical one and therefore more likely to renege on the promise.

To see how this phenomenon plays out in other realms, consider the case of a day-care center frustrated by parents who arrived late to pick up their children.[18] In an attempt to curb such late pickups, the center began requiring parents to pay a fine every time they picked up their children after hours. Problem solved? Not at all. In fact, more children were picked up late *after* the fine was instituted. Rather than decreasing undesirable behavior, the fine increased it. Why? Because the day-care center failed to account for the decision process of an individual faced with a fine. Suddenly, the ethical dimension of the problem was removed from parents' decision-making process. No longer did they view picking up their kids on time as the "right" thing to do. The fine caused them to focus their decision on the question of time versus money. In effect, late pickup became just another service being offered by the day-care center.

Note that in each of these contexts, the compliance system was a weak one without much teeth. The manufacturers could afford to pay the small fine, as could the parents who chose to stay a little longer at the office. A logical question would be whether it's only such weak compliance systems that exacerbate unethical behavior. In terms of our study, if the probability of getting caught were stronger and the fine were greater, participants would be less likely to renege on the agreement to run the scrubbers, right?

When we ran our study using a stronger compliance system, we did indeed find that reneging decreased.[19] However, we also discovered that, as in the case of the weak sanctioning system, most participants who were exposed to the strong sanctioning system saw it as a business decision, not an ethical one.

Why does it matter whether a compliance system leads to ethical fading if the desired results are achieved? The problem lies in what happens when the compliance system fails or is phased out. Returning to the day-care story, the center eventually removed the fine for late pickup; however, parents continued to pick up their kids late more often than they did before the fine was put into place. We've already seen that compliance systems tend to transform ethical decisions into business or practical decisions involving a calculation of the costs and benefits of compliance. This perspective remains even after the compliance system is removed. When a strong compliance system is dismantled, the costs of noncompliance become less onerous; the ethics have been faded from the decision, and the decision remains a practical one, with deviant behavior an attractive option.

Not only can compliance systems fail on their own, but individuals subjected to compliance systems often find ways to bring these systems down. Consider the phenomenon of "psychological reactance," or the common tendency to rebel against constraints on one's freedom. Psychologists have found that efforts to direct individuals' behavior often fail because individuals will devote extra effort to reclaiming their threatened freedom.[20] Forbidden fruit—whether video game privileges for children or a romantic interest who plays "hard to get"—becomes even more attractive when it's off limits. Compliance systems can have the same effect. When employees feel overly controlled, noncompliance may become more attractive simply because it's forbidden. To break free of the constraints created by compliance, employees may attempt to weaken, bypass, or trick the compliance system, determined to beat it at any cost.

While compliance systems can work, their failure rate is surprisingly high, often at great expense to employers. But the primary danger of compliance systems lies in their contortion of the decision-making process. Suddenly, instead of thinking about doing the right thing, employees focus on calculating the costs and benefits of compliance versus noncompliance—and about trying to outsmart the system.

How can an organization effectively head off unethical behavior rather than exacerbate it? As we will discuss, an examination of an organization's informal values through the lens of behavioral ethics will help to determine when compliance systems will work. Managers also need to guard against the trap of "forcing" ethics through monitoring, surveillance, and sanctioning systems. Promoting frameworks that highlight the ethical rather than the compliance dimensions of a decision will help ensure that employees are always cognizant of the ethical dimensions of any decision. In addition, leaders should encourage their staff to ask this important question when considering various options: "What ethical implications might arise from this decision?"

When Doing Good Becomes a License to Misbehave

We are aware of a number of not-for-profit organizations that are working hard to make the world a better place, yet mislead their constituencies about their success. They selectively provide data that make their organizations look better than reality suggests, and even manipulate data before releasing it to the public. These organizations are run by good people who likely would not mislead the public in a similar manner if they were running for-profit corporations. For example, they cannot be compared to cigarette industry executives who intentionally ran disinformation campaigns to confuse the public about the hazards of smoking. Rather, their focus on the good work they achieve appears to provide these leaders with an excuse to engage in dishonesty with the goal of raising more funds for their good causes. In chapter 1, we described an experimental study in which individuals had an opportunity to earn more money for themselves by cheating on the math puzzles they had been assigned to complete. Current research suggests that people are more likely to cheat on these tasks if they are earning money for charity than if they are earning money for themselves.[21]

Similarly, behavioral ethics research in the areas of moral compensation and moral equilibrium suggests that organizational efforts to promote ethical behavior can actually be associated with an *increase* in unethical behavior.[22] According to these theories, we each maintain a moral identity that we keep in balance by engaging in minor, compensatory moral behaviors. Because our moral behavior is dynamic, when we engage in a moral act, we may feel licensed to engage in immoral behavior in the future. Conversely, when we behave unethically, we may be motivated to behave more ethically in the future. For example, it has been found that reminding people of their humanitarian traits leads to subsequent reductions in charitable donations.[23] By contrast, when individuals violate their moral values, they are more likely to comply with requests for help.[24] Recent research conducted by Ann and her colleagues provides further evidence of this effect. In the study, some participants were asked to recall items that elicited a more positive moral self-image, such as the many things they did to contribute to environmental preservation or the few things they did to contribute to environmental destruction. These participants were significantly less likely to support programs to offset carbon dioxide emissions than were participants who were asked to recall items that elicited a less positive moral self-image (i.e., the many things they did to contribute to environmental destruction or the few things they did to contribute to environmental preservation).[25]

This finding relates to the example of disclosure of conflicts of interest. In chapter 5, we discussed the problem of conflicts of interest that arise when advisers, such as auditors, have misaligned incentives that cause them to condone unethical behavior or act unethically themselves. When scandals surrounding conflicts of interest arise, organizations, industries, or the government often respond by instating disclosure requirements that compel advisers to reveal the nature of their conflict of interest to their clients. The Sarbanes-Oxley Act, which requires corporations and the auditors that serve them to disclose their conflicts of interest, has been heralded as a means of achieving the goal of transparency and making companies more honest. Most people like the idea of requiring greater openness while still allowing professionals to act as they see fit. The well-intentioned focus on disclosure is based on the assumption that the public will benefit from increased information about an adviser's conflict of interest.

Unfortunately, disclosure isn't a fail-proof panacea for curbing unethical behavior. Not only do disclosure requirements fail to achieve their assumed objectives, they can actually have perverse effects on ethical behavior.[26] One interesting experiment reveals why. In the experiment, some participants, "the estimators," were asked to estimate the number of coins in a jar; other participants, "the advisers," were asked to advise the estimators as to the value of coins in the jar. The advisers were allowed to look more closely at the jar than estimators could. Estimators were paid according to the accuracy of their estimates. Some of the advisers were paid based on the accuracy of their estimator's estimate (after receiving the adviser's advice). Other advisers were paid based on how *high* their estimator's estimate was. Advisers in this condition faced a conflict of interest, as they would be rewarded not for their accuracy, but for estimate inflation. Not surprisingly, this latter group of advisers delivered higher estimates to their estimators than did the advisers who did not face a conflict of interest. More interesting, for our purposes, was what happened when the advisers disclosed their conflict of interest to their estimators: These advisers' estimates were higher and less accurate than those of other advisers; moreover, the estimators didn't discount the advice after learning of the conflict of interest. As a result, advisers actually earned more money, and estimators earned less money, when this conflict of interest was disclosed to estimators. In other words, disclosure actually *increased* the ill effects of the conflict of interest.

The goal of transparency is a rational one, yet it results in unintended consequences when we fail to account for the psychological process of moral compensation. In the study we've just described, disclosure apparently gave advisers a psychological license to severely overestimate the value of the coins. The opportunity to behave morally by disclosing a conflict of interest seems to give people a license to engage in future immoral behavior (inflated estimates, in this case) and therefore to maintain their moral equilibrium.

Managers and other decision makers can mitigate the deleterious effects of moral compensation through the separation of ethical and unethical standards, a zero-tolerance policy for unethical behavior, and standards for ethical behavior that are continually adjusted upward. Moral compensation is significantly less likely when leaders communicate to employees that unethical behavior is distinct and separate from ethical behavior and when they set a separate standard for the two. For example, setting a zero-tolerance standard for unethical behavior, while at the same time setting standards for honest reporting, makes it more difficult for employees to attempt to mitigate unethical behavior through good deeds. Similarly, by continually raising the bar for ethical behavior, organizations make it more difficult for employees to settle in on a comfortable "ethical balance."

The Domination of Informal Cultures

In the 1980s, Ann's father worked on the management side of management-union negotiations in the wholesale food industry. He would come home with colorful stories of the negotiations, describing in particular how union leaders would grandstand in front of their constituents, promising to fight management on any and all concessions and bring home a victory. Management, he admitted, would present an equally tough stance, steadfast about the need for concessions and their ability to fight to the bitter end. Behind closed doors, however, the theatrics ended. Union and management representatives would turn to each other and politely ask, "What will it take to settle this?"

As this anecdote illustrates, organizations' public, formal norms are often at odds with the informal, often hidden cultures that guide employees' behavior. Like formal policies and communications, informal organizational cultures send signals regarding acceptable behavior, including ethical behavior.[27] Formal ethics programs, such as codes of conduct, ethics training, and mission statements, tend to be well documented. By contrast, the signals conveyed through informal cultures do not come from official pronouncements or actions; rather, they are "felt" by organizational members.[28] Carrying messages that are heard but not seen, informal cultures represent the unofficial messages regarding ethical norms within the organization. It is through informal mechanisms that employees learn the "true values" of the organization.

Consider the case of an actual company that had a formal code of

conduct that exhaustively described the ethical standards that its employees were expected to meet. The code of conduct was deemed so important
that all employees were instructed to read the manual and then sign a
"Certificate of Compliance" form. That should do the trick, right? Unfortunately, at Enron, it did not.

Like Enron, Johnson & Johnson has well-established codes of conduct
(see figures 7 and 8).[29] Why, then, have we witnessed such dramatic differences between these two companies in terms of ethical behavior? Differences in the length and content of the two documents are probably not to
blame. More likely, the real difference can be traced to the informal cultures in which these formal systems were embedded. Johnson & Johnson
is widely known for its ethical culture, the best-known example being the
company's voluntary recall of Tylenol during the 1982 cyanide-tainting
crisis, a decision estimated to have cost the company $100 million.[30] In
this company, its formal code of ethics was consistent with its informal
culture. (Some would argue that a recall of numerous Johnson & Johnson
medicines in 2010 suggests that this informal culture has lapsed, despite
the continued existence of the credo.) By contrast, Enron became notori-
ous for its underlying culture of greed and competition. The company's
sophisticated, lengthy formal code of conduct was no match for its unethical informal culture.

Ann and her colleagues Kristin Smith-Crowe and Elizabeth Umphress argue that formal systems are the weakest link in an organization's ethical infrastructure and are typically far eclipsed by their informal counterparts.[31] Ralph Larsen, the former CEO of Johnson & Johnson,
expressed a similar opinion when he told the *National Journal*, "All the
laws in the world cannot ensure that corporate executives will observe
them day in and day out."[32] Indeed, one study of employee deviance in
the retail, health care, and manufacturing industries found that the formal controls of managers were inferior to the informal social controls
imposed by coworkers.[33] Anthropologists argue that such informal systems can be traced to our evolved mental capacity for social organization;

by contrast, because formal systems have no evolutionary roots, they are artificial and less influential.[34] In groups, informal norms have been identified as the initial forces that guide transactions and other activity. Only as groups grow larger and more diverse do formal mechanisms (such as contracts and codes of conduct) emerge to facilitate their activities.[35]

Sometimes formal systems are weak because they were purposefully designed to be that way. Specifically decoupled from the organization's "true" inner workings, codes of conduct can be mere attempts to convince outsiders, and particularly investors, that the organization is ethical while disguising its more important goals, such as profit maximization. Research on annual reports offers some support for this perception. Firms that use ethics-related terms such as "ethics" and "corporate responsibility" in their 10-K annual reports are more likely to be associated with "sin" stocks, or publicly traded companies involved in producing alcohol, tobacco, and gaming. Notably, firms using ethics-related terms in these reports are also more likely than other firms to be the object of class-action lawsuits and to score poorly on corporate governance measures.[36] Apparently, companies in need of a good disguise rely on "ethics marketing" in their annual reports.

If a corporation were truly concerned about its ethics, would it carefully craft compliance systems and codes of ethics designed to address its unique structure and problems, or would it simply borrow the systems and codes of another organization? Interestingly, plagiarism of an ethics code could be a sign that an organization's ethical aspirations may be nothing more than window dressing. One study that compared corporate codes of ethics found substantial levels of similarity in sentences and content.[37] In a sample of the Standard & Poor's 500 Index, the average firm had about 37 sentences in its code of ethics that were repeated word for word in other S&P 500 codes. For some codes, the overlap was 222 sentence matches! One of the most common sentences—"Theft, carelessness and waste have a direct impact on the company's profitability"—was

Our Credo

We believe our first responsibility is to the doctors, nurses and patients,
to mothers and fathers and all others who use our products and services.
In meeting their needs everything we do must be of high quality.
We must constantly strive to reduce our costs
in order to maintain reasonable prices.
Customers' orders must be serviced promptly and accurately.
Our suppliers and distributers must have an opportunity
to make a fair profit.

We are responsible to our employees,
the men and women who work with us throughout the world.
Everyone must be considered as an individual.
We must respect their dignity and recognize their merit.
They must have a sense of security in their jobs.
Compensation must be fair and adequate,
and working conditions clean, orderly and safe.
We must be mindful of ways to help our employees fulfill
their family responsibilities.
Employees must feel free to make suggestions and complaints.
There must be equal opportunity for employment, development
and advancement for those qualified.
We must provide competent management,
and their actions must be just and ethical.

We are responsible to the communities in which we live and work
and to the world community as well.
We must be good citizens—support good works and charities
and bear our fair share of taxes.
We must encourage civic improvements and better health and education.
We must maintain in good order
the property we are privileged to use,
protecting the environment and natural resources.

Our final responsibility is to our stockholders.
Business must make a sound profit.
We must experiment with new ideas.
Research must be carried on, innovative programs developed
and mistakes paid for.
New equipment must be purchased, new facilities provided
and new products launched.
Reserves must be created to provide for adverse times.
When we operate according to these principles,
the stockholders should realize a fair return.

Johnson & Johnson

Figure 7. Johnson & Johnson Credo. Reprinted with permission from Johnson & Johnson.

Business Ethics

Employees of Enron Corp., its subsidiaries, and its affiliated companies (collectively the "Company") are charged with conducting their business affairs in accordance with the highest ethical standards. An employee shall not conduct himself or herself in a manner which directly or indirectly would be detrimental to the best interests of the Company or in a manner which would bring to the employee financial gain separately derived as a direct consequence of his or her employment with the Company. Moral as well as legal obligations will be fulfilled openly, promptly, and in a manner which will reflect pride on the Company's name.

Products and services of the Company will be of the highest quality and as represented. Advertising and promotion will be truthful, not exaggerated or misleading.

Agreements, whether contractual or verbal, will be honored. No bribes, bonuses, kickbacks, lavish entertainment, or gifts will be given or received in exchange for special position, price, or privelege.

Employees will maintain the confidentiality of the Company's sensitive or proprietary information and will not use such information for their personal benefit.

Employees shall refrain, both during and after their employment, from publishing any oral or written statements about the Company or any of its' officers, employees, agents, or representatives that are slanderous, libelous, or defamatory; or that disclose private or confidential information about their business affairs; or that constitute an intrusion into their seclusion or private lives; or that give rise to unreasonable publicity about their private lives; or that place them in a false light before the public; or that constitute a misappropriation of their name or likeness.

Relations with the Company's many publics—customers, stockholders, governments, employees, suppliers, press, and bankers—will be conducted in honesty, candor, and fairness.

Figure 8. Enron code of ethics. Courtesy of the Department of Justice. http://www .justice.gov/enron/exhibit/02-06/BBC-0001/Images/EXH012-02970.PDF

traced to an identical sentence in a New York Stock Exchange regulatory document that specifies the topics a company's codes should address. Worse yet, there were some cases of complete ethics code duplication. Formal systems that are borrowed from another firm, rather than reflecting the specific values of an organization, are a shallow overlay with relatively little impact.

Oftentimes, formal compliance programs are weak not because of flaws in their design, but because they are overshadowed by the organization's informal culture. The power of informal cultures to trump formal systems is clearly illustrated in the demise of Enron and Arthur Andersen. In what one observer described as a "quiet dilution of standards and the rise of auditor-salesman," "bluntly honest" auditors within Andersen, particularly those associated with the firm's Professional Standards Group (the "watchdog group" designed to keep its audits honest) were belittled and denigrated, such that they took on second-class status.[38] When a former partner of Andersen's Ethics and Responsibilities Business Practices consulting services brought up the subject of internal ethics, she said she "was looked at as if [she] had teleported in from another world."[39]

At the headquarters of Enron, Arthur Andersen's most powerful client, a similar story unfolded. CEO Kenneth Lay made it clear that informal rules trumped formal codes of conduct, wrote reporter Alexei Barrionuevo in the *New York Times*:

> Ethical rules that he had helped set up at Enron, including the company code of conduct, somehow did not apply to him, Mr. Lay suggested. When questioned . . . about a $160,000 personal investment he made in a photo-sharing company that did more than 80 percent of its business with Enron, Mr. Lay called suggestions of impropriety "form over substance." Rules, he said, "are important, but you should not be a slave to rules, either."[40]

In contrast to formal norms and rules, informal norms are difficult to overtly identify. Rather, they are embedded in the stories employees tell, the euphemisms they use, the socialization methods they encounter, and the informal enforcement of norms. Consider Ann's experience as a new professor at Notre Dame University. When she was moving into her office, numerous students offered to help her with her boxes. She politely declined their kind offers, but the students were so insistent that she finally acquiesced. The students not only opened doors for her, but carried boxes to her office and then followed her to her car to see if they could help with more. Ann appreciated the generosity of this assistance, but couldn't help but wonder if it was motivated by the fact that she is a short woman and was clearly struggling with the boxes.

About two years later, Ann heard a colleague in her department describe the move-in experience of another colleague—a man who was anything but short and appeared to be quite strong. Just like Ann, the male colleague reportedly had been amazed by the offers of help. Later, Ann jokingly accused her colleague of stealing "her" box story, only to learn that he truly had experienced the same generosity. Together, these stories powerfully reveal the informal values that characterize Notre Dame. "Help professors carry boxes" cannot be found in any student handbook; rather, these norms are made visible and salient through stories repeated in informal conversations.

Informal norms don't even require a complete story to become ingrained in an organization or society. The words we choose to describe, or disguise, behaviors can be just as effective. In his sketch "They're Only Words," the comedian George Carlin traces the evolution of the term used to describe the effects of battle stress on soldiers.[41] Labeled "shell shock" in World War I, the term became "battle fatigue" in World War II, only to morph into "operational exhaustion" in the Korean War, and finally "post-traumatic stress disorder" (or PTSD, for short) during the Vietnam War. Through humor, Carlin argues that as the term has been sanitized over time, it has buried soldiers' pain under jargon and made it easy for society to ignore the issue.

In a similar manner, organizations attempt to mask their unethical behavior by cloaking it in innocuous language. "Collateral damage" is more acceptable than "dead civilians," and "earnings management" and "creative accounting" are less bothersome terms than "cooking the books." Nuclear radiation is measured by "sunshine units," pollution becomes "runoff," and chemical waste is "by-product." Employees are "laid off," "downsized," and "made redundant," but they are rarely fired. Disguising the brutality of harmful behavior with soft language makes the unacceptable permissible and allows unethical practices to abound. In addition to perpetuating unethical behavior, euphemisms send a powerful informal signal about an organization's values to its employees: As long as you disguise and hide your unethical behavior, we will accept it, and indeed even encourage it.

In addition to absorbing informal norms through stories and euphemisms, we pick up on them by observing which behaviors are rewarded and which are not. A lawyer in a prestigious law firm told the story of a group of junior associates who were having dinner together. The group included three junior associates who were performing up to expectations and another junior associate who was the firm's "golden boy"—a star performer who was getting choice assignments and working with the best partners in the firm. Junior associates, like all members of law firms, have to bill their hours in increments and assign them to specific billing codes. As we have noted, because the list of codes can be exhaustive, accurately accounting for one's time in such detail is often difficult, requiring lawyers to keep copious notes and constantly record their hours on their time sheets. During dinner, as the moderately performing associates were discussing the time-consuming nature of the billing process, the star associate pulled out his timesheet and quickly filled it in for several weeks, without referring to any notes on how he had spent his time. It was obvious to the other associates that this star's reporting wasn't particularly accurate or truthful. Formal policies clearly specified accurate billing procedures, and the list of billing codes had been carefully reviewed with the associates. Yet the cavalier actions of the star left these formal rules in the dust.

Like formal rules, informal norms are reinforced not only with rewards but also with sanctions, often with much more alarming results.

Take one of the world's largest makers of cast-iron water and sewer pipes, McWane. The company's informal sanctions are seen as incredibly influential and largely responsible for the company's reputation as "one of the most dangerous businesses in America."[42] In 2003, in an industry that had the worst safety record, McWane held the title for the highest employee injury rate, and with good reason: between 1995 and 2003, McWane had been cited for more than 400 safety violations, four times more than its six major competitors combined. Having been found in violation of pollution rules and emission limits at least 450 times during that same time period, McWane plants also have been identified as among the worst polluters in New Jersey, Alabama, and Texas. Supervisors are said to routinely ignore safety and environmental laws that conflict with production, going so far as to dump polluted water in the dark of night. Informal sanctions within the company reportedly allow these practices to perpetuate. Workers who protest working conditions are "bull's-eyed," or marked for termination. Injured workers are bullied, and union leaders are intimidated.

The following anecdote, reported in the *Chicago Tribune*, reveals that the enforcement of informal norms—in this case, the norm that stealing is to be tolerated—can be quite extreme in organizations:

> The voice on the police line was firm but halting: "OK. I'd like to report an employee theft which is gonna occur at James River [paper mill] . . . I witnessed ah, him, you know, loading the stuff up . . . to take it out . . . but, he, ah, ah, he's known to be violent." After a five-day suspension for refusing to cooperate with an investigation of the reported theft, the [accused] employee, Keith Kutska, legally acquired a recording of the call. Then he took it to work, "because people wanted to know who the snitch was," he said at a hearing. "I played it and said, 'There he is.'" One day later, on November 22, Monfil's [the accuser's] body was found at the bottom of a 20-foot holding vat for tissue pulp. A jump rope attached to a 40-pound weight was tied to his neck.[43]

The influence of informal systems within organizations is not lost on Hector Sants, the chief executive of Britain's financial industry regulatory body, the Financial Services Authority (FSA). In the wake of the 2008 financial crisis, interviewees for senior banking jobs with the FSA are now being subjected to a much stricter interview process, one that includes an assessment of their ability to foster an ethical culture. Executives are evaluated based on how they treat customers and their ethical behavior in the marketplace. "Our aim would therefore be to seek to facilitate the creation of good cultures and intervene when bad ones seem to be creating unacceptable outcomes," Sants told the *New York Times.*"[44]

This practice suggests a potentially useful means of improving the ethicality of informal cultures within organizations. Leaders should inventory the informal systems that exist and work to understand the underlying pressures that are put on employees. Such pressure points can come from existing reward systems, from other employees, and from supervisors. By focusing on the underlying cultures that may counteract formal systems, leaders may be able to make strides toward creating positive informal cultures that reinforce ethical behavior and shun unethical behavior.

Although organizational efforts to create systems that improve members' ethical behavior are often well intentioned, psychological processes limit the effectiveness of such solutions. Unless leaders take individuals' actual decision processes into account, employees and citizens in general will largely ignore these systems or even increase their unethical behavior. In table 1, we summarize the barriers presented in this chapter and describe possible steps you and your organization can take to cope with them. Designing effective systems to promote ethical behavior in organizations requires an understanding of the obstacles that are likely to arise and a set of strategies to overcome them.

Table 1

Designing Effective Systems to Promote Ethical Behavior in Organizations

Barriers	What problems can arise?	Issues to consider
Reward systems	Reward systems don't consider the means to which people may go to achieve the goals or the potential impact on other goals.	When setting goals, brainstorm all of the side-effects of achieving the stated goal. Involve those who are actually being rewarded and ask them to identify the likely behaviors that will result.
Sanctioning systems	Punishing unacceptable behavior encourages ethical fading and increases the probability that the behavior will be evaluated via a cost-benefit analysis rather than on its ethicality.	Include ethical assessments when making decisions related to personnel, strategy, or operations. Make sure that the question "What ethical implications might arise from this decision?" is asked routinely when considering various options.
Moral compensation	Ethical acts can be used as justification for unacceptable behavior in another domain.	Have separate standards for ethical and unethical behavior. Set a zero-tolerance policy for unethical behavior. Set high expectations for ethical behavior and stress the importance of continually raising ethical standards.
Informal systems	Informal cultures and peer pressure can dominate well-intended formal ethics systems.	Inventory the organization's informal systems and work to understand the underlying pressures on employees. Strive to create positive informal cultures that reinforce ethical behavior and shun unethical behavior.

Chapter 7

Why We Fail to Fix Our Corrupted Institutions

One of the most obvious means of saving human lives would be to eliminate deaths caused by tobacco.[1] Tobacco killed about 100 million people in the twentieth century and is projected to kill as many as a billion people in the twenty-first century.[2] Yet despite the brave efforts of those who have stood up to the tobacco industry over the last sixty years, our society, and specifically the U.S. government, has done and continues to do shockingly little to avoid these deaths. Our elected officials have been corrupted into inaction, but the vast majority of us fail to notice or complain.

Across a variety of domains, including regulation of the tobacco industry, regulation of the auditing industry, and management of climate change, for-profit organizations, not-for-profit organizations, and the U.S. government have repeatedly failed to act to maximize the interests of society. In each case, corporations intentionally have acted to distort how citizens and legislators understand the issue and to prevent not-for-profit organizations and the government from intervening on citizens' behalf. However, our interest is not in the illegal behaviors of some of these industries or the legal but corrupting influences of their disinformation campaigns.[3] Nor will we repeat the important argument that government policies are distorted by the unique ability of special-interest group to harness their resources to influence policy (in other words, the argument that it is easier for several tobacco companies to agree on a policy preference and combine resources than it is for 300 million citizens to do so). Rather, using the perspective of behavioral ethics, we will focus primarily on the failure of politicians and other professionals to notice, confront, and overcome these corrupting influences and on the failure of citizens to hold elected officials accountable for suboptimal policies. In chapter 5, we explored the common failure to notice the unethical actions of others; this chapter examines how we fail to notice and act on the corruption of government policy.

A fundamental goal of any government should be to enlarge the pie of resources that society has at its disposal. Yet when government decisions are crafted to benefit small groups of constituents, valuable public resources—ranging from tax dollars to fisheries to the global climate—are often misused and ignored, and the pie of available resources shrinks. We will explore the intersection between psychological processes and political systems to understand why citizens and legislators allow this phenomenon to occur.

When the pot of resources is as large as it can be without making others worse off, economists consider it to be "Pareto-optimal." A Pareto-optimal change is one that provides greater benefits for some and makes no one worse off. At the national and international level, Pareto-optimal changes are nonexistent, since any change will cause harm to someone, somewhere. The Nobel Prize–winning economist Joseph Stiglitz argues that some trade-offs are "near-Pareto improvements."[4] These policies create large benefits for many people while imposing comparatively small losses upon others, such as a special-interest group that may have already manipulated the political system to its advantage. Stiglitz argues that "if everyone except a narrowly defined special-interest group could be shown to benefit, surely the change should be made."[5] Unfortunately, society often fails to make such near-Pareto policy improvements.

Ideally, changes to government policy should entail wise trade-offs— trades in which gains significantly exceed losses for most citizens.[6] Thus, for a new tobacco policy to be wise, its expected value to society, in terms of lives saved and disease prevented, should be larger than the costs to tobacco companies and citizens (such as shareholder value and loss of enjoyment from smoking). When virtually everyone but a narrowly defined special-interest group is expected to benefit from a policy, that policy is a wise one.[7]

Why does the U.S. government so often fail to enact such wise policies? To understand why, we will explore the failure of the government to act to reduce the corruption of policy in three industries: tobacco, auditing, and energy. Of course, many other issues—such as U.S. government subsidies and the U.S. educational policy—fit into the same pattern of dysfunction, but we chose three issues where the record of corrupted institutions is quite clear. For each case, we will briefly describe the barriers to wise policy created by the interplay between political systems, the interests of a small number of actors who benefit from contorting policy to their own narrow goals, and the psychological processes of the citizens who bear the brunt of the policy outcomes. Our main focus will concern our failure as a society to end this destructive corruption.

Big Tobacco

According to archaeological evidence, Mayans smoked tobacco as early as the first century B.C.[8] Although tobacco was native to the Americas, Christopher Columbus's exposure to the plant led to the early diffusion of smoking in other parts of the world. Tobacco was banned in China as early as 1612 and then in Berlin in 1723. The big boom in smoking came with the branding of cigarettes in the middle to late 1800s, and specifically with the 1880 invention of the Bonsack cigarette-rolling machine, which could produce 100,000 cigarettes per day.[9]

The first suspicions about a link between tobacco and cancer date back to 1761. By 1858, extremely strong correlational evidence emerged between pipe smoking and cancer of the mouth. Over the next one hundred years, evidence of a connection between smoking and cancer accumulated. A link to lung cancer had been suggested by 1912, and such theories became common by the 1920s. The first quantitative analysis connecting cigarettes and lung cancer appeared in 1929; it showed that lung cancer victims were much more likely to be smokers than nonsmokers were.[10]

A critical question remained: Did cigarettes cause cancer, or did some other determinant of cancer create a correlation between smoking and cancer? For example, if people who lived in environmental conditions that caused cancer also smoked more than those in other areas, then it would be conceptually possible for a correlation between smoking and cancer to exist without pinpointing smoking as the agent that caused the cancer.

Significant research to determine whether smoking actually caused cancer followed the 1929 study. By the early 1950s, many quantifiable studies existed, and causal studies with nonhuman animals had been conducted. In 1957, the British Medical Research Council formally blamed tobacco for the growth of lung cancer throughout society. The London Royal College of Physicians concluded in 1962 that steps were needed to curb the rising consumption of tobacco. Finally, in 1964, the U.S. surgeon general publicly concluded that smoking was causally related to lung cancer.[11] By then, it was apparent that smokers were approximately twenty times as likely to contract lung disease as nonsmokers.

What should we have known by when? Medical historians who haven't been paid for their opinions by the tobacco industry generally argue that a clear consensus emerged among scientists on the causal role of tobacco on lung cancer by the early 1950s.[12] But this information remained hidden from the public, thanks to the cigarette industry's advertising and lobbying efforts. During this time, the tobacco industry not only continued to produce an addictive product, it hid its own research on the causal connection between cigarettes and lung cancer, actively targeted underage smokers in its ad campaigns, and did a fantastic job of keeping Congress from creating laws and regulations that would impede sale of tobacco products.

Why did the U.S. public fail to push legislators on initiatives such as opposing the marketing of cigarettes to underage smokers? In large part it was because the tobacco companies conducted a very effective disinformation campaign to create doubt in the public's mind about the causal effect of tobacco on lung diseases. Historian Robert Proctor coined the term "agnotology" to describe the cultural production of ignorance (as opposed to knowledge) and cited the actions of the tobacco industry as a prime example of corporate interests conspiring to create agnotology. Specifically, the tobacco industry consistently told the public that there was no conclusive proof of a link between smoking and cancer, that there were many other potential causes of cancer, and that further research was needed. Tobacco company executives counted on the fact that it would be nearly impossible to determine whether smoking was the agent that caused cancer. In addition, as is usually the case after a scientific consensus emerges on a controversial topic, "experts" were paid to offer their skeptical opinions. For all of these reasons, until the surgeon general weighed in on the matter on 1964, it was reasonable for the public to be confused about the health risks of tobacco products.

These tactics were successful in part because they played on the psychological processes of the leaders of the American Medical Association and other doctors. Throughout the research developments that occurred from 1929 through the 1950s, and even after the surgeon general's report was released in 1964, Big Tobacco found a strong ally in organized medicine, the community that understood medical science far better than most other citizens. At the time the surgeon general's report was released and in the years that immediately followed, the American Medical Association (AMA) was concerned about pending legislation to create Medicare and Medicaid, which it perceived as a threat to doctors' fees. The AMA wanted to avoid alienating legislators from tobacco-growing states, as they would soon be voting on these and other important health-care reform issues of the 1960s. Thus, the AMA refused to take a position on the harms of tobacco and even followed the tobacco industry's lead in calling for more research on the matter—research that all parties involved knew was unnecessary to reach a clear conclusion. Perhaps as a result of ethical fading, the AMA viewed the tobacco issue through a business lens rather than an ethical lens; the health of citizens remained out of focus when the group made its decisions. Journalists Drew Pearson and Jack Anderson later described the coalition between the medical and tobacco industries as "the weirdest lobbying alliance in legislative history."[13]

What about individual doctors? What would prevent them from accepting the powerful evidence that was available about the causal connection between cigarettes and lung cancer? In an example of the motivated blindness phenomenon we described in chapter 5, perhaps it was doctors' own cigarette habits that limited them from seeing the clearly available evidence. Harvard historian Allan Brandt documents that in 1954, 52 percent of physicians reported being regular smokers; 30 percent reported smoking at least a pack of cigarettes a day. In 1959, as the science connecting tobacco to lung cancer continued to develop, 39 percent of doctors remained regular smokers, with 18 percent smoking at least a pack a day.[14] Evarts Graham, a prominent surgeon who transformed himself from a skeptic to a leading figure in the antismoking movement, argued this point about the link between cigarette smoking and lung cancer as early as 1954:

> [The link] has not been universally accepted and there are still many cigarette addicts among the medical profession who demand absolute proof. The obstinacy of many of them in refusing to accept the existing evidence compels me to conclude that it is their own addiction to this drug habit which blinds them. They have eyes to see but they see not because of their unwillingness or inability to give up smoking. . . . I have never encountered any non-smoker who makes light of the evidence or is skeptical of the association between excessive smoking and lung cancer.[15]

Thus, at the same time that the tobacco industry spent millions of dollars actively and effectively lobbying Congress and supplying misinformation to the public, a community that should have been protecting us from these efforts, the medical establishment, had been effectively corrupted, probably without the key actors recognizing the harm they were perpetuating.[16]

Tobacco products currently kill about 500,000 Americans per year and about five million people worldwide, a figure that is growing. Had the medical community taken the responsible position of emphasizing the causal role between tobacco and lung cancer, citizens would have been less confused by the tactics of the tobacco industry, and millions of lives might have been saved. Are we saying that the AMA and individual doctors intentionally killed their patients? No. Rather, their ability to see the clear evidence was affected by their focus on defeating Medicare and Medicaid, their own addiction, and their lack of insight into how these preferences blinded them to the evidence. As a result, millions of people have died and will die terrible, premature deaths.

The Auditing Industry

The future of the [accounting] profession is bright and will remain bright—as long as the Commission does not force us into an outdated role trapped in the old economy. Unfortunately, the proposed rule [on auditor independence] threatens to do exactly that. A broad scope of practice is critical to enable us to keep up with the new business environment, attract, motivate and keep top talent, and thereby provide high quality audits in the future.

—Joseph Berardino, managing partner, Arthur Andersen, in written testimony provided for the SEC's hearing on auditor independence, July 26, 2000

In chapter 5, we discussed the collapse of Enron and its auditor, Arthur Andersen, in light of Andersen's failure to act on the shocking level of corruption that occurred at Enron. Here we turn to the question of why our society allowed—and still allows—a corrupt auditing system to exist in its current form.

The Securities and Exchange Act of 1934 established mandatory independent audits of publicly traded companies in order to give third parties confidence that the companies' books could be trusted. Unfortunately, fatal flaws were built into the act. From the start, the accounting firms that were hired to conduct audits had an incentive to curry favor with the same companies whose books they were supposed to examine without bias. The act failed to include measures that were needed to create truly independent audits: (1) required assignment rotation of auditors, such that auditors would not be biased toward retaining a client; (2) prohibition of auditors from selling consulting and other services to their clients; and (3) prohibition of auditors from taking jobs with the firms they audited.[17]

At the same time, independence was largely viewed as central to the institution of auditing. Chief Justice Warren Burger wrote in a unanimous Supreme Court ruling in the case of the *United States v. Arthur Young & Co.* (1984):

> By certifying the public reports that collectively depict a corporation's financial status, the independent auditor assumes a public responsibility transcending any employment relationship with the client. The independent public accountant performing this special function owes ultimate allegiance to the corporation's creditors and stockholders, as well as to the investing public. This "public watchdog" function demands that the accountant maintain total independence from the client at all times and requires complete fidelity to the public trust.

Nonetheless, by the 1980s, accounting firms had begun to supplement the relatively low margins of their competitively priced audits with more profitable tax, management, and technology consulting contracts. With auditing partners under increasing pressure to sell consulting services to their audit clients, an atmosphere developed in which accountants were increasingly dependent on their clients for approval. "Part of the [annual salary] evaluation was how well you generated new business," said former SEC chief accountant Lynn Turner of his days as an auditor at Coopers & Lybrand in the 1990s. "If someone brought in $25 million in consulting fees, they were a hero." In a 1996 report, the Government Accounting Office commented that the expansion of consulting services posed a risk to auditors' independence.

In the late 1990s, SEC chairman Arthur Levitt became concerned about auditors' independence as a result of a series of scandals. In the summer of 1998, for example, the SEC learned that executives at Price Waterhouse (now PricewaterhouseCoopers) had been investing in companies their firm was auditing, in direct violation of SEC rules; more than 8,000 violations were uncovered within the firm. The SEC fined Price Waterhouse $2.5 million, and Levitt made auditor independence his top priority as SEC chairman. Given the lack of accountability and the potential for a huge disaster, the solution, Levitt believed, was a clean break between auditing and consulting duties. But Levitt was shaken by a joint meeting he held with executives from three of the largest accounting firms—KPMG, Deloitte & Touche, and Arthur Andersen. Levitt later paraphrased the executives: "We're going to war with you. This will kill our business. We're going to fight you tooth and nail. And we'll fight you in the Congress and we'll fight you in the courts."[18]

The accounting firms engaged no fewer than seven lobbying firms to fight the auditor independence proposal. Levitt received many dozens of letters in support of the accounting industry's stance from corporate executives and congressmen; in particular, Representative Billy Tauzin of Louisiana "badgered me relentlessly," Levitt said.[19] In a letter to Levitt dated September 20, 2000, Enron chairman Kenneth Lay attested to the benefits his energy-trading company had received from one-stop shopping with Arthur Andersen: "Enron has found its 'integrated audit' arrangement to be more efficient and cost-effective than the more traditional roles of separate internal and external auditing functions."[20] In fact, it later emerged that David Duncan, the Andersen partner in charge of Enron's audits, had cowritten Lay's letter with help from Andersen's Washington lobbying firm.[21] During this period, Enron was Andersen's second-largest client, providing not only its annual audit, but also tax, business-consulting, and internal audit services.[22] In 2000, the year of Levitt's battle, accounting firms donated more than $10 million to national political campaigns and spent another $12.6 million on federal lobbying, according to the Center for Responsive Politics.[23]

In 2000 Levitt also welcomed expert witnesses from government, corporations, accounting firms, and academia to Washington to testify in

SEC hearings on the issue of auditor independence. Max and his colleague George F. Loewenstein, the Herbert Simon Professor of Economics and Psychology at Carnegie Mellon University, were among those who
presented their opinions on auditor independence to the SEC. In a 1997
Sloan Management Review article with Kimberly P. Morgan entitled "The
Impossibility of Auditor Independence," we argued that focusing solely
on auditors' neglect and corruption when evaluating the repercussions of
accounting scandals was a mistake. Auditor bias arises at the unconscious
stage where decisions are made, long before auditors report their judgments. For this reason, we declared that audit failures are a natural
by-product of the auditor-client relationship and that the current U.S.
audit system makes it "psychologically impossible," because of motivated
blindness, for even the most honest auditors to make objective judgments; "cases of audit failure are inevitable," we wrote.[24]

In our written SEC testimony in 2000, we backed measures to separate the auditing and consulting functions of accounting firms, but also
stressed that unbiased audits would be unlikely as long as auditors continued to be hired and fired by the companies they audit. With our colleague Don Moore, a professor at the Haas School of Business at the
University of California at Berkeley, we have since argued that, to create
both the appearance and reality of true auditor independence, the following reforms are needed:

1. Auditing firms should only provide auditing services to their
   clients.
2. Auditing contracts should be of a limited duration, during which
   time the client should not be allowed to fire the auditor.
3. Companies should be prohibited from hiring accountants who
   have audited their books.[25]

As we noted earlier, these three issues were overlooked by the Securities
and Exchange Act of 1934. Levitt was convinced of the potential danger of
auditors' conflicts of interest. His goal for the SEC hearings was to convince Congress to listen to us and other witnesses instead of to the ac-

counting industry lobbyists. At the hearings, Arthur Andersen managing partner Joseph Berardino, KPMG vice president J. Terry Strange, and Deloitte & Touche partner Robert Garland demanded the SEC provide evidence of past instances of audit fraud caused by auditing firms' consulting business. "Given what is at stake," Garland testified, "and the fact that there is no demonstrated problem, it would be irresponsible to take on the considerable risks surrounding the proposed rule."[26] According to Strange, "Nonaudit services improve audit effectiveness."[27] "In our opinion, we do think [the proposal] will harm audit quality," said Berardino. "The more the auditors know about their client the better the audit is," he argued further. "If you or I were a CEO and wanted to perpetrate a fraud or cook the books, I think we'd want to keep the auditors in the dark. I don't think we'd be hiring them to help us implement our [information technology] systems. I don't think we'd be helping them to look at our complex transactions.[28]

After the hearings, key legislators sided with the auditing firms. According to Levitt, Representative Tauzin "knew what the accountants were doing before I did. He was working very closely with them. I don't mean to sound cynical, but is it because he loves accountants?"[29] As it turns out, Tauzin received more than $280,000 in campaign contributions from the accounting industry in the 1990s, though he had never faced a serious challenger for his House seat.[30] Even worse, Levitt learned that House Appropriations Committee member Henry Bonilla was ready to slash the SEC's budget by attaching a rider to the commission's appropriations budget if Levitt didn't back down on the issue of auditor independence.[31]

Reluctantly, Levitt gave up the fight—a decision he later called his biggest mistake as SEC chief.[32] Convinced he would eventually be defeated by Congress, he allowed accounting firms to continue to perform consulting work for their audit clients. The firms made just one concession: they agreed to disclose the details of these relationships to their investors. Notably, research that we reviewed in an earlier chapter shows that disclosure can actually *exacerbate* bias.[33] Levitt understood that disclosure was an inadequate solution to the problem of auditors' conflict of interest, but he believed it was the only measure Congress would pass.

We all know what happened next. Enron crashed as a result of its spectacular misdeeds, which had gone unreported by its auditor, Arthur Andersen. Andersen, blamed for turning a blind eye to Enron's corruption because of its reliance on the company for hefty consulting contracts, soon went bankrupt as well. Subsequent accounting scandals in the first half of 2002 were connected to the failures at WorldCom, Adelphia, Global Crossing, Xerox, and Tyco.

In response to these scandals, President George W. Bush signed the Sarbanes-Oxley Act into law on July 3, 2002. Sarbanes-Oxley imposed a variety of reporting requirements on public companies that many senior executives viewed as excessive government regulation. By contrast, left-leaning critics considered the new regulations to be insufficient.

From our own point of view, Sarbanes-Oxley utterly failed to respond to the key flaws of the auditing industry. Sarbanes-Oxley prohibited auditors from providing some consulting services, but allowed other audit services to continue. Sarbanes-Oxley required rotation of the accountant who leads an audit after seven years, but not rotation of the audit firm itself (a last-minute changed lobbied for by the "Final Four" accounting firms). In addition, auditors are still permitted to take jobs with the firms they audit. Lest we worry about the profitability of the Final Four firms in the post-Sarbanes-Oxley era, they ironically are making up some of their lost opportunities by providing Sarbanes-Oxley compliance services. These firms succeeded at lobbying Congress to avoid meaningful, promising reforms that would affect their profitability. Fueled by the egocentrism described in chapter 3, legislators acted unethically by focusing on how reforms would affect their own campaign contributions, rather than on the costs incurred by a very significant societal problem. In addition, because the impact of this institutionalized corruption felt distant to citizens, the media and average citizens gave the issue too little attention, contributing to an environment ripe for future disasters.

It is noteworthy that the larger corporate world hasn't been particularly interested in improving auditors' independence. Honest corporations make many decisions that depend on the integrity of the financial statements of other firms. Thus, honest corporations would benefit from more accurate and forthright accounting. But these corporations are also subject to audits, and in some cases, they benefit from "flexible" auditing and from having their own auditors provide consulting and other services. Consistent with our argument in chapter 3 about discounting the future, many corporate leaders don't want to interrupt their current one-stop shopping relationship with accounting firms in exchange for the longer-term benefits of being able to trust the books of other firms. So they keep quiet and ignore the long-term implications of inaction for their corporations and society at large.

In late 2009, reflecting on the past decade, economist and *New York Times* columnist Paul Krugman highlighted the importance of having an honest auditing system by quoting from a speech that Lawrence Summers gave in 1999 as the deputy Treasury secretary under President Clinton (as of 2010, Summers is the Obama administration's top economist).[34] "If you ask why the American financial system succeeds," Summers said, "at least my reading of the history would be that there is no innovation more important than that of generally accepted accounting principles: it means that every investor gets to see information presented on a comparable basis; that there is discipline on company managements in the way they report and monitor their activities." It is now clear that we, as a society, failed in our ethical obligation to create and maintain the type of ethical system of accounting that Summers believed in and praised. And in March 2010, with Big Four accounting firm Ernst & Young facing blame in the collapse of Lehman Brothers, it appears that the U.S. auditing system continues to fail us.[35]

The Energy Industry

Global climate change was identified as an emerging problem in the 1930s, after a long period of warm weather. Interest in the issue dissipated when cooler temperatures returned. Decades later, scientists provided clear evidence of melting glaciers and other massive environmental change that indicated widespread climate change. As a scientific consensus emerged, the issue of climate change became almost impossible to ignore.

Most of the rare scientific skeptics who do remain are paid for their views by the oil, coal, and automotive industries. ExxonMobil has emerged as the most prominent and generous funder of research designed to discredit climate-change claims.[36] A 2007 report released by the Union of Concerned Scientists documented that, between 1998 and 2005, ExxonMobil funneled about $16 million to a network of ideological and advocacy groups that work to stir up false uncertainty on the climate-change issue. The organizations supported by the oil company publish non-peer-reviewed work by a small group of "scientific spokespeople." The Union of Concerned Scientists report accuses ExxonMobil of "actively propping up discredited studies and misleading information that would otherwise never thrive in the scientific marketplace of ideas."[37] As an example, physicist Frederick Seitz earned more than $585,000 in the 1970s and 1980s as a paid consultant to R. J. Reynolds Tobacco Company and became an outspoken climate-change skeptic in the 1990s. Seitz has been paid by several organizations hostile to climate-change regulation, including the George C. Marshall Institute, which received $630,000 from ExxonMobil between 1998 and 2005.[38] Yet in an interview with PBS's show *Frontline*, Seitz insisted that the money he received from both the oil and tobacco industries did not influence his scientific findings.

During the same period it was supporting known climate-change skeptics, ExxonMobil also funded more established research institutions that seek to better understand climate change through true scientific methods, most notably through a $100 million grant to help Stanford University's Global Climate and Energy Project study new energy technologies aimed at lowering greenhouse gas emissions. The Union of Concerned Scientists report notes:

This seemingly inconsistent activity makes sense when looked at through a broader lens. Like the tobacco companies in previous decades, this strategy provides a positive "pro-science" public stance for ExxonMobil that masks their activity to delay meaningful action on global warming and helps keep the public debate stalled on the science rather than focused on policy options to address the problem.[39]

In 2006, the American Enterprise Institute (AEI), a think tank that had received more than $1.6 million from ExxonMobil, offered scientists and economists $10,000 each for articles that would undermine an impending report from the UN's Intergovernmental Panel on Climate Change (IPCC).[40] The most comprehensive review of climate change to date, the IPCC report predicted that global average temperatures would continue to rise over the next century and stated that there was a 90 percent likelihood that human action was to blame. After the report was released, ExxonMobil did an about-face; CEO Rex W. Tillerson joined competitors BP and Shell in acknowledging that greenhouse gases from automotive and industrial exhausts contribute to global warming. In addition, the AEI reportedly pulled back on its plan to pay scientists for articles critical of the report.[41] The IPCC received the 2007 Nobel Peace Prize for its report. Yet researchers supported by the energy industry continue to dispute the well-established data that climate change is ongoing and perpetuated by humans.

"There isn't any scientific principle according to which all alarming possibilities prove to be benign upon further investigation," wrote Nobel Prize–winning economist Thomas Schelling in 1984. Yet despite the widespread consensus on the issue and the alarming predictions, a surprising number of politicians and voters, both in the United States and in other industrialized and developing countries, largely ignore the climate change problem, insist it is not real, or make only symbolic or costless moves to address it. This is due in part to the fact that the costs of addressing climate change are significant. Developing economies, such as China and India, would suffer massive economic loss if they were required to reduce their reliance on fossil fuels. Many employees would lose jobs, and many more would need to change their lifestyles.

Despite these considerable costs, the current scientific consensus is that they are likely to be far lower than the eventual catastrophic costs of inaction.[42] Ocean levels and weather patterns are predicted to dramatically change the climate of some areas. Glaciers will melt, oceans will rise, and disastrous consequences are in store for coastal areas and low-lying countries such as Bangladesh. Islands and coastlines across the globe are expected to become uninhabitable, and dikes will have to be built to protect cities and agricultural land. Millions of people likely will be forced to relocate, while others may have to reorganize their systems of farming. Net food production is expected to decrease.[43]

Many nations signed on to the 1997 Kyoto Protocol, which called for the return of greenhouse emissions to 1990 levels by the year 2010; the United States, however, did not. The protocol did not achieve its stated objectives and may never be fully implemented. In 2009, despite high hopes, the United Nations climate change negotiations in Copenhagen failed to secure the critical commitments necessary to appropriately address the climate-change challenge. The original goals of the Copenhagen talks were to reach a binding treaty that would mandate concrete, verifiable global action on climate change. But, marred by protests and power struggles, the talks only produced short-term, nonbinding promises. The participating nations merely agreed to "take note" of a three-page pact that promised financing for developing nations and created a reporting and monitoring system of the greenhouse gas emissions of wealthier nations. At Copenhagen, Secretary of State Hillary Clinton announced that the United States would contribute its share of the annual $100 billion in long-term financing needed to help poor nations adapt to climate change, but this promise is conditioned upon congressional approval—hardly a sure thing.[44]

A legislator who supports measures aimed at reducing climate change can expect little support from his constituents, especially if the cost of doing so includes new taxes on SUVs, gasoline, electricity, and so on. As we argued in chapter 6, reward systems within organizations direct employees' attention toward achieving particular goals, thus causing them to ignore other important goals. The rewards offered under our political system create similar problems. The goal of many politicians is reelection. The general public's tendency to discount the future and avoid even minor inconveniences hinders us from endorsing the actions of politicians who accept the need to inflict small costs in the present to avoid future catastrophe. If the constituents who are most influential in a politician's reelection (such as deep-pocketed campaign donors) fight policies aimed at confronting climate change, politicians have an incentive to side with them and to subvert the public interest.

Overall, the failure to respond effectively to climate change can be viewed as a massive pattern of unethical behavior committed not only by our elected officials, but by us ordinary citizens. This failure can be attributed not only to the costs of addressing the issue, but also to the cognitive biases we discussed in chapter 3. More specifically, as Max wrote in a 2006 article, cognitive biases lead us to (1) have positive illusions that reduce our tendency to focus on problems, such as climate change, that loom in the distant future, (2) interpret events such as climate change in a self-serving manner and to view others, rather than ourselves, as responsible for the problem, (3) try desperately to maintain the status quo and refuse to accept any costs, even when those costs would bring about a greater good and prevent future harm, and (4) fail to invest in preventing problems, such as climate change, that we have not personally experienced or witnessed through vivid data.[45]

Different Problems, Similar Strategies

Institutional corruption is a condition that exists when our institutions (governments, corporations, and not-for-profits) formalize a set of policies and practices that weaken the effectiveness of society and the public's trust in these institutions, even if no law is broken, according to Larry Lessig, the director of the Safra Center for Ethics at Harvard University. Society institutionalizes corruption by enacting laws and regulatory systems that can be predicted to fail to maximize societal interests. As a prime example, corrupted institutions exist when we and our elected officials allow special-interest groups to distort public policy for their own benefit through disinformation campaigns.[46]

Responsibility rests at least partially on those of us who unknowingly allow corrupt institutions to perpetuate. To halt their unethical behaviors, we need to replace our ignorance with informed understanding. Throughout this book, we have used the lens of behavioral ethics to document the psychological processes that lead to unethical actions and, using the three examples in this chapter, have linked those processes to the behavior of those in our political system. The next step is to uncover the tactics that political and corporate actors use so that their force can be mitigated.

Many of these tactics, which we will describe below, play on the status quo bias, or the common preference for maintaining an established behavior or condition rather than changing it.[47] Psychologists have long known that, when contemplating a potential change, we tend to be more concerned about the risk of change than about the risk of failing to change. Imagine, for instance, that you receive an offer for a job that is much better than your current job on some dimensions (pay, responsibility, etc.) and marginally worse on others (location, health insurance, etc.). A rational analysis would imply that if the evident gains exceed the expected losses, you should accept the new job. However, the psychological tendency to pay more attention to losses than to gains will lead many to turn down the job, preserve the status quo, and forgo a net gain.[48] Because losses loom larger than gains, the status quo creates inertia that is a barrier to wise action.[49]

In chapter 1, we attributed the *Challenger* disaster to a failure of NASA and Morton Thiokol engineers to look outside the bounds of the data available to them in the room the night before the launch. A secondary explanation for this disaster can be traced to NASA manager Larry Mulloy's successful argument that no change to the decision to launch the next day should be made without strong scientific evidence. In this manner, he implanted the decision to launch as the status quo in the minds of those present. This framing went against the more appropriate standard of choosing not to launch until safety was reasonably assured. Mulloy's positioning helped move the decision in the boundedly unethical direction of launching the shuttle.

The powerful desire to maintain the status quo is partly responsible for the continued existence of corrupt institutional processes. Moreover, those who are the most harmed by current systems are sometimes the most vocal advocates of these systems, note psychologists John Jost and Mahzarin Banaji.[50] Smokers are often slow to complain about the tactics of the tobacco industry, corporations that are damaged by the corrupted annual reports of other firms remain silent, and the poor—who are least able to adapt to climate change—may rank this issue low on their list of priorities. By justifying existing systems, we perpetuate a harmful status quo, often unwittingly.

The status quo bias interacts with a set of tactics used again and again by special-interest groups opposed to wise policy change. Specifically, those who oppose action on the issues we have identified—tobacco, auditing, and climate change—systematically rely on three techniques: (1) obfuscation and the encouragement of reasonable doubt, (2) the claimed need to search for a smoking gun, and (3) shifting views of the facts. Whenever the U.S. government has been on the verge of making a significant change in these realms, these techniques effectively increased the impact of the status quo on its decisions.

Obfuscation and the Encouragement of Reasonable Doubt

Corporations that want to delay governmental response on an issue important to them use a key tool that has worked for decades: obfuscation, or the practice of communicating in a deliberately confusing or ambiguous manner with the intention of misleading the listener. The main goal of obfuscation is to create reasonable doubt about change in the minds of citizens and policymakers and thus to encourage the status quo to prevail.

The U.S. tobacco industry knew far more about the hazards of cigarette smoking than the public health community did.[51] In addition, Big Tobacco maintained an explicit strategy of creating doubt in the mind of smokers about the health effects of cigarettes long after there was scientific clarity about the causal role of cigarettes in lung cancer. This strategy of promoting reasonable doubt in the minds of consumers lasted for forty years, from the 1950s to the 1990s.[52] To avoid or slow down antismoking measures, the tobacco industry has also stirred up confusion about the known deleterious effects of secondhand smoke. As early as 1981, convincing evidence existed that secondhand smoke was related to lung cancer. A Japanese study found that wives of smokers and ex-smokers were much more likely to get lung cancer than were wives of nonsmokers, and that the risk was significantly related to the amount of smoking by their husbands.[53] Yet the tobacco industry fostered doubt about this research in the minds of the public, long after a scientific consensus emerged on the ill effects of secondhand smoke.

Similarly, the auditing industry argued that its high ethical standards answered concerns about the structure of the U.S. auditing system. In response to strong evidence from SEC chairman Arthur Levitt and others that consulting services compromised the independence of audits, the major auditing firms, like the credit-rating agencies in the 2008 financial crisis, claimed their integrity protected them, thereby creating reasonable doubt in the minds of politicians and the public about the need for change.

Finally, the coal, oil, and automotive industries have engaged in obfuscation concerning the existence of climate change and the role of humans in creating the problem. Even after a clear consensus existed among scientists who were not being paid for the views, the oil and coal industries spent enormous amounts of time and money communicating to the public that some experts doubted the existence of climate change and, if it did exist, the role that humans played in perpetuating it.

All three groups were well aware that obfuscation creates uncertainty. Their carefully planted seeds of doubt have made it difficult for politicians to act and for citizens to mobilize in support of reform. After all, who wants to pay the costs if change isn't really needed?

The Search for a Smoking Gun

Which of the following proposals do you think is more likely to lead to an independent auditing system?[54]

1. To achieve auditor independence, prohibit auditors from establishing durable long-term cooperative partnerships with their clients, from providing nonaudit services to their clients, and from taking jobs with their clients.
2. Begin with a variety of incentives that motivate auditors to want to please their clients. Next, try to identify a complex set of legislative and professional incentives to counteract the corrupting influences created by the desire to please the client.

We think the answer to this question is pretty clear. Obviously, it makes more sense to begin with a truly independent system than to add patches to an existing, corrupt system. Yet the auditing industry argued in public SEC hearings that there was no clear evidence that auditors' conflicts of interest were a problem, and that without a smoking gun, no change was warranted.

Have we convinced you that auditors should not be rehired by their auditing clients, that auditors should not be allowed to provide other services to firms they audit, and that auditors should not be allowed to take jobs with their clients? Unfortunately, Max and his colleague George Loewenstein did not convince the SEC when they testified in 2000. Its commissioners wanted to know if we could identify a "smoking gun"—a specific audit that was clearly biased because the auditing firm had provided other services to its client. The SEC commissioners were looking for an e-mail message or memo that would provide clear evidence of knowing and intentional corruption. We could not provide such evidence. Furthermore, in their testimony, the CEOs of three of the big accounting firms noted that there was no evidence of a single audit being tainted as a result of the auditing-consulting relationship. While such evidence may sometimes emerge (as it did later in 2000, in a case involving Arthur Andersen and Waste Management), proving that a particular case of audit fraud was caused by nonaudit services is as challenging as proving that a particular smoker's lung cancer is caused by smoking or that a particular heat wave is caused by climate change; any single case is complicated by numerous confounding factors.

A smoking gun should not be needed to reach the conclusion that massive changes were, and still are, needed to create true auditor independence, optimal regulation of smoking, and an effective response to climate change. When we wait for a smoking gun, we typically wait too long and fail in our duty to enact better policies for society. When the institutions that guide the behavior of key actors are corrupted, we should act long before a disaster occurs.

Expressing Shifting Views of the Facts

The forces that oppose wise reforms typically present their own distorted view of the "facts." When their positions become untenable and maintaining the status quo is impossible, these groups simply change their position and deny their past connection to claims that they now acknowledge, in the face of overwhelming evidence, to be clearly false. For decades, the tobacco industry held fast to the view that cigarettes caused no harm, and indeed might even help smokers achieve positive health benefits, such as weight control, improved digestion, and relaxation. As the scientific connection between lung cancer and cigarettes mounted, the industry grudgingly acknowledged that cigarettes might be one of many possible causes of lung cancer, but, clinging to the status quo as long as they could, insisted that no specific cancer could be traced to cigarettes and that the causal path was unclear. To manage its changing story, soon after seven tobacco CEOs testified to Congress in 1994 that cigarettes caused cancer, the industry quickly replaced all seven CEOs. After finally admitting that cigarette smoking caused lung cancer, in a breathtaking about-face, Big Tobacco argued that smokers who contract lung cancer should not be allowed to sue the industry for damages, since it was public knowledge that tobacco might be harmful—this, despite the industry's well-funded disinformation campaigns across the decades and its persistent attempts to turn teenagers into addicts.

In a similar manner, the U.S. auditing industry transitioned from the view that its sterling reputation protected it from conflicts of interest to the view that, if a problem existed, disclosure would be an effective response. When it became clear that disclosure had failed and that regulatory changes appeared feasible, the auditors changed their views again. Now they focused on whether solving the theoretical problem of independence would be worth the cost. Of course, this argument ignored the basic point that if audits are not independent, they have no reason to exist in the first place.

As for the issue of climate change, after years of obfuscation, the oil, coal, and automotive industries have made a relatively rapid shift in recent years: from insisting that manmade global warming did not exist, to claiming that global warming is not caused by human actions, to arguing that it would not be worth the enormous costs to fix the problem.[55] By maintaining the most reactionary view that is defensible and shifting their positions only out of necessity, the enemies of wise policies succeed in delaying change and profit during the delay.

What Can We Do?

Psychologists tend to study the individual, while political scientists generally study political institutions. In our earlier chapters, drawing on behavioral ethics theory and research, we focused on the biases that create bounded ethicality at an individual level. Identifying these biases is the first step toward reducing our bounded ethicality. In this chapter, we have tried to highlight the interplay between these two forces—the personal and the political—by highlighting how they lead to outcomes that, if we could remove our blind spots, we would deem to be unacceptable for society. In the next chapter, we move toward a broader consideration of how the behavioral ethics perspective can helps us achieve a more ethical society.

Chapter 8

Narrowing the Gap
Interventions for Improving Ethical Behavior

You might be surprised to learn that Ann and Max (the authors) do not agree on a number of ethical issues. In fact, we disagree on lots of policy issues with ethical implications. We do not share identical philosophical perspectives. Nor do we have religious perspectives in common; one of us is a churchgoing Catholic, the other a nonreligious Jew. As a result, we've had to negotiate about some of the stories that made it into the earlier chapters, and some that did not.

Our differences may help to explain why we haven't tried to impose either of our ethical standards on you. At the same time, we recognize that our own perspectives and values probably influenced the examples we used. We have no interest in encouraging you to act according to our or anyone else's ethical values. Rather, our goal is to help you, others, and organizations make the ethical decisions you would make upon thoughtful, reasoned reflection.

We have offered up seven chapters' worth of evidence from behavioral ethics that people do not act as ethically as they would upon deeper reflection. In this chapter, we turn our attention to the concept of change: that is, how you can use the knowledge acquired in earlier chapters to bring your own decisions in closer alignment with your ethical views, and how you can help the organizations to which you belong—and society in general—do the same.

Changing Yourself

> Only the wisest and stupidest of men never change.
>
> —Confucius

Given that few people number among the wisest and the stupidest of society, virtually all of us are ripe for change, according to Confucius's standards. Yet change can be difficult, and changing our ethical behavior can be particularly tough. As we have tried to document, we believe much of this difficulty rests in a lack of awareness of the negative ethical implications of our actions.

So, when it comes to improving your ethical behavior, what's an individual to do? The answer lies in part in aligning the gap between your "want" and "should" selves. As argued in chapter 4, we tend to predict that we will behave as we think we *should* behave, but at the time of the decision, we behave how we *want* to behave. To make matters worse, when we reflect back on the decision, we tend to believe that we acted as we thought we *should* behave.

Most of us understand that to make an effective decision, we need to engage in thorough deliberation prior to the decision and, after making the decision, accurately reflect on it.[1] However, because our predictions of how we will behave aren't accurate, we have trouble making the ethical decisions we planned to make. Moreover, because we distort our recall of decisions to help us feel better about any unethical behavior we may have committed, our reflections aren't accurate, either. As Max and his colleague Mahzarin Banaji have argued, to make ethical decisions, you need to recognize your vulnerability to your own unconscious biases.[2] If you don't, you won't be aware of your blind spots.

One of the first steps toward removing your blind spots is to make sure you are planning appropriately and reflecting realistically on your behavior. As we described in chapter 4, System 1 refers to our fast, automatic, effortless, implicit, and emotional decision processes, while System 2 refers to slower, conscious, effortful, explicit, logical, and more reasoned decision processes. Our intuitive System 1 responses are more likely to be immoral than our more reflective System 2 thoughts.[3] This would suggest that learning to think before acting, in more reflective and analytical ways, would help us move toward the ideal image we hold of ourselves. Doing so entails being prepared for the hidden psychological forces that crop up before, during, and after we confront ethical dilemmas.

Preparing to Decide: Anticipating the "Want" Self

The "want" self—that part of us which behaves according to self-interest and, often, without regard for moral principles—is silent during the planning stage of a decision but typically emerges and dominates at the time of the decision. Not only will your self-interested motives be more prevalent than you think, but they likely will override whatever "moral" thoughts you have. If you find yourself thinking, "I'd never do that" and "Of course I'll choose the right path," it's likely your planning efforts will fail, and you'll be unprepared for the influence of self-interest at the time of the decision.

One useful way to prepare for the onslaught of the "want" self is to think about the motivations that are likely to influence you at the time you make a decision, as Ann and her colleagues have demonstrated in their research.[4] Drawing on the sexual harassment study discussed in chapter 4, participants were asked to predict how they would react if a job interviewer asked questions that qualified as sexual harassment. Participants who were induced to think about the motivation they likely would experience at the time of the decision—the desire to get the job—were significantly less likely to predict that they would confront the harasser and more likely to predict that they would stay silent (just as those in the actual situation did) than were those who were not asked to think about the motivation they would experience at the time of the decision. As this study suggests, thinking about your motivations at the time of a decision can help bring the "want" self out of hiding during the planning stage and thus promote more accurate predictions.

To help our negotiation students anticipate the influence of the "want" self on decisions that have an ethical dimension, we ask them to prepare for the very question they hope won't be asked. When preparing for a job negotiation, for example, we encourage them to be ready to field questions about other offers they may have. Otherwise, when a potential employer asks "What's your other salary offer?" an applicant's "want" self might answer "$90,000," when the truthful answer is $70,000. If an applicant has prepared for this type of question, her "should" self will be more assertive during the actual interview, leading her to answer in a way that's in harmony with her ethical principles, yet still strategic: "I'm afraid I'm not comfortable revealing that information."

Similarly, rehearsing or practicing for an upcoming event, such as a work presentation or exams, may help you focus on concrete details of the future situation that you might otherwise overlook.[5] In her book *Giving Voice to Values*, Mary Gentile offers a framework to help managers prepare for difficult ethical decisions by practicing their responses to ethical situations.[6] When you are able to project yourself into a future situation, almost as if you were actually in it, you can better anticipate which motivations will be most powerful and prepare to manage them.

The point of increasing your accuracy in the planning stage of decision making isn't to recognize that you will be influenced by self-interested motives and admit defeat to the "want" self. Rather, it's to arm you with accurate information about your most likely response so that you can engage in proactive strategies to reduce that probability. Knowing that your "want" self will exert undue pressure at the time of the decision and increase the odds that self-interest will dominate can help you use self-control strategies to curb that influence.[7]

One such strategy involves putting in place precommitment devices that seal you to a desired course of action.[8] In one example, Philippine farmers who saved their money by putting it in a "lockbox" that they could not access were able to save more money than those who did not, even factoring in the small cost of the lockbox.[9] By eliminating the farmers' ability to spend their money immediately, the lockbox effectively constrained the "want" self. Ann's teaching assistant used a similar pre-commitment strategy to constrain her "want" self during finals week. Knowing she should study but would be tempted to procrastinate by spending time on Facebook, she had her roommate change her password so that she could not access the social networking site. By doing so, the student constrained her "want" self from acting and allowed her "should" self to flourish. Such precommitment devices explain the popularity of personal trainers at health clubs. By making appointments with a trainer (who might charge up to $100 an hour) with the threat of a cancellation fee, clients precommit to their "should" self, ensuring that they will work out rather than giving into the strong pull of the "want" self and watching TV instead.

When faced with an ethical dilemma, we can use similar strategies to keep our "want" self from dominating more reasoned decision making. Research on the widespread phenomenon of escalation of commitment—our reluctance to walk away from a chosen course of action—shows that those who publicly commit to a decision in advance are more likely to follow through with the decision than are those who do not make such a commitment.[10] You might also precommit to your intended ethical choice by sharing it with an unbiased individual whose opinion you respect and whom you believe to be highly ethical. In doing so, you can induce escalation of commitment and increase the likelihood that you will make the decision you planned and hoped to make.

Making the Decision: Giving Voice to Your "Should" Self

In addition to preparing for the power of the "want" self at the time of decision, there are other ways to give more power to the "should" self. For instance, given that abstract thinking dominates our thinking when we are predicting how we will behave, it's useful to bring this abstract think-ing to light when we are actually making a decision as well. Focusing on the high-level aspects of the situation at the time of the decision may be one way to do this.[11] For example, a group of researchers was able to reduce the immediate temptation of eating a tasty pretzel by refocusing participants' attention away from the concrete aspects of the temptation—how good the pretzel would taste—and toward the abstract dimensions; they did so by asking participants to imagine that they were looking at a picture of a pretzel rather than an actual pretzel.[12] Similarly, in the famous "marshmallow experiments," a child was placed alone in a room with a single marshmallow on her plate.[13] An adult told the child that she had only two choices: (1) eat the marshmallow before the adult came back to the room, in which case she would only get that one marshmallow, or (2) wait to eat the marshmallow until after the adult returned and be rewarded with a second marshmallow for her patience. (For a demonstration of this experiment, visit www.blindspots-ethics.com/temptation.) The success of the "temptation resistors" seemed to rest at least partly on the level of thinking in which the children engaged. Those who were encouraged to think about vivid and highly arousing pictures of the marshmallow quickly succumbed to temptation and ate it, while children who were encouraged to think about the marshmallows as abstract images (for example, as a puffy cloud) were more likely to resist temptation and wait for the reward.[14]

In a similar manner, when we are faced with an ethical dilemma, we may be able to give the "should" self a stronger voice by focusing on the abstract principles that guide the decision. Rather than thinking about the immediate payoff of an unethical choice, thinking about the values and principles that you believe should guide the decision may give the "should" self a fighting chance. A useful strategy for encouraging abstract thinking is to imagine the eulogy you would like written about you and your actions. What principles will people say guided your life? What would you like them to say?

Still find yourself thinking of the trees and not the forest? If so, the "mom litmus test" may be useful. When faced with a tempting but possibly unethical choice, ask yourself whether you would feel comfortable sharing that decision with your mom (or your dad or someone else you really respect). Could you comfortably approach your mother and say,

"Guess what, Mom? I lied about having another salary offer in order to get the job." Imagining your mom's reaction in that exchange is likely to bring abstract principles to mind ("What would Mom do?") and thus give the "should" voice more power.

Yet another efficient strategy for drawing attention to the "should" self involves changing the decision set from that of a single option— "Should I behave unethically or not?"—to a choice between options. Based on their research, Max, Ann, and their colleagues have argued that the "should" self tends to dominate if decision makers have the chance to evaluate more than one option at a time.[15] For example, individuals who evaluated two options at a time—an improvement in air quality (the "should" choice) and a commodity such as a printer (the "want" choice)— were more likely to choose the option that maximized the public good (improvement in air quality); by contrast, when participants evaluated these options independently of one another, they more often chose the printer.[16] Similarly, in a choice between two political candidates, one of higher integrity and one who would provide more jobs, individuals who evaluated the two candidates side by side voted for the higher-integrity candidate; when participants evaluated the candidates independently, the one who provided more jobs was more popular.

This evidence suggests the value of joint decision making when assessing ethicality or making ethical judgments, consistent with long-standing advice in the decision literature to consider all available alternatives when making decisions. Reformulating an ethical dilemma into a choice between two options—the ethical choice and the unethical choice—should be helpful in bringing the "should" choice to the forefront, highlighting the fact that by choosing the unethical action, you are *not* choosing the ethical act.

One might argue that the recommendations presented—think abstractly, apply the "mom test," and construe the decision as one involving more than one option—require an awareness that a decision has an ethical component. Of course, if that were the case, these recommendations wouldn't be needed in the first place! Rather, ethical decision making requires that we apply these recommendations to all of our important decisions.

Evaluating Your Unethical Choice—Accurately

The desire to be an ethical person is a noble aspiration, yet ironically, it can actually impede your ability to accurately assess your unethical behavior and behave more ethically in the future. As discussed in chapter 4, because we want to see ourselves as ethical (and have others see us that way as well), our recollections of our behavior are biased in that direction—that is, we're predisposed to reinterpret our unethical behavior as ethical. Unfortunately, "debiasing" ourselves of this tendency is quite hard.[17]

Because it can be so difficult, people tend to need training to help them identify and correct the distorted feedback they give themselves. Rather than focusing on how they *should* behave, such training should emphasize the psychological mechanisms that lead to unethical behavior and inaccurate recollections of such behavior.[18] In addition, it needs to incorporate techniques to help people to accurately recall their behavior. Training individuals on the biases and distortions that impede accurate evaluation of their actions and asking them to examine reasons their initial recollection might be wrong can help mitigate the effects of these biases.[19]

Decision feedback is another effective means of improving your ability to accurately assess your actions. Feedback needs to be immediate, and it should warn about the likelihood of distortions and describe how bias might affect your recollection of the decision.[20] Debriefing your decisions on a regular basis, perhaps with the help of a trusted friend or colleague playing the part of "devil's advocate," may also help improve the accuracy of your recollections. Perhaps because they have built-in feedback mechanisms, group decision making and systems that hold people accountable for their decisions are other effective methods of debiasing judgment.[21]

Changing Organizations

> When it was discovered the gas tank was unsafe, did anyone go to
> Iacocca and tell him? "Hell no," replied an engineer who worked on
> the Pinto, a high company official for many years, who, unlike
> several others at Ford, maintains a necessarily clandestine concern
> for safety. "That person would have been fired. Safety wasn't a
> popular subject around Ford in those days. With Lee it was taboo.
> Whenever a problem was raised that meant a delay on the Pinto, Lee
> would chomp on his cigar, look out the window and say 'Read the
> product objectives and get back to work.'" . . . Iacocca was fond of
> saying, "Safety doesn't sell."[22]
>
> —Douglas Birsch and John H. Fielder, *The Ford Pinto Case*

As this quotation suggests, closing the ethical gap in an organization requires a thorough audit of top leaders' decisions and behavior. Lacking a
leader who believes in ethical decision making, an organization won't
behave ethically. But while having an ethical leader is a necessary quality
of an ethical organization, it is by no means sufficient. Findings from behavioral ethics suggest that less obvious, hidden aspects of unethical behavior also need to be addressed, including the organization's informal
values and ethical "sinkholes," which are characterized by decision uncertainty, employee stress, and the isolation of decision makers.

Identifying Hidden—but Powerful—Informal Values

An organization may espouse ethical values, require ethical training, and
even have an ethics "hotline," yet such symbolic moves may have relatively little impact on ethical behavior.[23] As we argued in chapter 6, the
informal values imparted at work play a much more critical role in employee behavior. If they want to see real ethical improvement in their organizations, managers need to understand these informal values. Doing
so requires an understanding of the processes that motivate individual

employees' decisions. What pressures do employees feel and why? What ethical challenges do they face? What types of decisions does the organization actually reward? What qualities characterize those who make it to the top?

One way to get to the heart of these questions is to try to identify who really "runs the company"—which may not necessarily mean the CEO. In the later days of Arthur Andersen, it was the consultants who had the most power. At Ford during the Pinto era, it was the salesmen: "This company is run by salesmen, not engineers; so the priority is styling, not safety," said one Ford engineer.[24] Identifying these pockets of power can reveal a great deal about the true values of the organization. If winning consulting business is an accounting firm's penultimate goal, what considerations are pushed aside to achieve it? If salesmen are running an auto manufacturer, whose voices are silenced?

While the question of who's in charge depends upon the organization, chances are that a consensus will exist within each organization. In universities, it's generally known which colleges "have the president's ear." In companies, employees tend to know which departments are "the place to be seen and heard"—that is, where you need to land if you want to make it to the top. On the flip side, employees are also aware of the "dead zone"—the departments where no one wants to land—which also reveals the company's true priorities.

Paying attention to "organizational talk" can also shed light on the informal values at work. Noticing what's talked about—and what isn't—can shed light on the values that employees believe are actually rewarded, as well as those that aren't. What slogans and stories do employees repeat over and over? What values do those stories emphasize? As an internal company slogan, "Safety doesn't sell" sends an incredibly powerful message about what is and isn't important to the organization. In doing so, it blocks certain criteria from employees' decision-making process—specifically, in this case, eliminating customer safety as a consideration. In this manner, the ethics of considering the potential effects of one's decisions on others' well-being fades from the decision process.

Stories are a particularly powerful mechanism for alerting employees to the informal values of their organizations. Is there company lore about someone who stood up to leadership on an ethical issue—for example, an engineer "taking on Iacocca" over the Pinto? Or is the story one of being rebuffed by a leader for mentioning ethical concerns? Both types of stories would powerfully reveal an organization's true values and cause employees to hold very different beliefs about expected behavior and decision criteria.

One well-known client of ours, a Fortune 50 corporation, produced a video of four stories told by four employees who went above their bosses' heads to keep the corporation from acting unethically. Each tells his or her story in vivid detail and stresses that he or she was simply doing what was needed to behave ethically. The video is widely shown within the organization. At the end of the video, we learn that all four whistleblowers now hold very senior positions in the corporation. While it's true that a formal decision was made to create the video, it has had a lasting, powerful effect because the stories are repeated through informal channels.

Paying attention to what *isn't* talked within an organization also provides valuable information about its informal values, as exemplified in this quote from Barbara Toffler, a former Arthur Andersen employee:[25] "We were supposedly still the guardians of the public trust, but no one ever mentioned that. Everyone did, however, talk about making money all the time." Similarly, an anonymous Ford engineer's story concerning gas-tank safety at the auto company, as recounted by Douglas Birsch and John H. Fielder in their book *The Ford Pinto Case*, provides a compelling demonstration of the importance of considering the "popularity" of certain topics and their relationship to organizational values:

> Lou Tubben is one of the most popular engineers at Ford. He's a friendly, outgoing guy with a genuine concern for safety. By 1971 he had grown so concerned about gas-tank integrity that he asked his boss if he could prepare a presentation on safer tank design. Tubben and his boss had both worked on the Pinto and shared a concern for

its safety. His boss gave him the go-ahead, scheduled a date for the presentation and invited all company engineers and key production planning personnel. When time came for the meeting, a grand total of two people showed up—Lou Tubben and his boss.[26]

The anonymous Ford engineer who related this story ironically commented, "So you see, there are a few of us here at Ford who are concerned about fire safety," and added, "They are mostly engineers who have to study a lot of accident reports and look at pictures of burned people. But we don't talk about it much. It isn't a popular subject."[27]

As this story suggests, "ethics talk"—or lack thereof—also reveals a great deal about an organization. How are unethical behaviors described? More importantly, how are they disguised? For example, when someone is found to have lied to management or to a customer, is the word "lying" used, or is the behavior disguised as "misrepresenting the facts"? Is stealing described as an "inappropriate allocation of resources"?[28] The importance of labeling is exemplified in a study in which participants had a sensible aversion to eating from a container labeled "cyanide."[29] Interestingly, participants had trouble overcoming this impulse even when they themselves were the ones to write "cyanide" on an otherwise clean container. There is similar power in calling unethical behavior by its name. If unethical behavior isn't labeled as such, it is unlikely that an intervention will be attempted, let alone that one will succeed.

Because informal values are organization-specific, ethics "fixes" will depend on those values and be unique to each organization. As we have discussed, formal systems such as codes of conduct and ethics training don't drive informal values; rather, informal values need to drive which formal systems are warranted and how they are designed. An organization cannot simply "borrow" another organization's formal ethics plan, as so many do; nor can the government mandate particular programs and expect success. Identifying the informal values that drive an organization is difficult and may reveal unpleasant truths, yet organizations that truly desire meaningful change must undertake this hard work.

Identifying Ethical "Sinkholes" in the Organization

The difficult task of identifying how an organization's informal values differ from its desired ethical values can be made easier by identifying characteristics that make misalignment more likely. More specifically, paying attention to areas in the organization that are characterized by uncertainty, time pressure, short-term horizons, and isolation serves as a good first start.

Uncertainty is a catalyst for the ethical fading process, Max, Ann, and their colleague David Messick have found.[30] Namely, the more uncertainty there is the environment, the more likely unethical behavior is to occur. In addition, in her research, Ann found that individuals were more likely to lie about the amount of resources they had to allocate to another person when the recipient was uncertain about the actual amount available. In environments characterized by high uncertainty, individuals may be able to downplay the ethical implications of a decision and, in doing so, become more likely to code the decision as a business choice rather than an ethical one. Uncertainty also has been identified as a catalyst in the divergence between the "want" and "should" self. By introducing the idea that an outcome may not have ethical implications, the "want" self may be able to focus on its own desires, increasing the probability that the individual will make an unethical act choice.[31] In the case of the Ford Pinto, focusing on the likelihood that the gas tank wouldn't combust upon impact fades other possible outcomes—combustion and subsequent loss of life—from consideration, allowing the decision to be recoded as a business rather than an ethical decision.

Time pressure within an organization is another likely source of unethical behavior. The busier and more rushed people are, the more they have on their minds, and the more likely they are to rely on System 1 thinking. In particular, the frantic pace of managerial life suggests that executives often rely on System 1 thinking.[32] Notably, time pressure characterized the production of the Ford Pinto. Described as "the shortest production planning period in modern automotive history," the Pinto's production schedule was set at under twenty-five months, an aggressive timeline given the average production schedule of forty-three months.[33] Time pressure reduces the cognitive resources available to decision makers and decreases their odds of making "should" choices. In a study examining consumer choice, individuals who were asked to memorize a seven-digit number were more likely to choose chocolate cake over fruit salad (i.e., the "want" choice), whereas those who only had to memorize a two-digit number were more likely to choose the fruit (i.e., the "should" choice).[34] We can increase our likelihood of making a "should" choice by analyzing ethical dilemmas in an environment free of distractions and time pressures.

Isolation also tends to promote informal values that are at odds with an organization's desired values. Isolated individuals and groups tend to develop norms that diverge from the stated norms of the organization. From 1990 to 1994, for example, General Electric paid fines ranging from a $20,000 criminal fine to a $24.6 million civil fine for employees' unethical behaviors that included misrepresentation, money laundering, defective pricing, cost mischarging, false claims, product substitution, conspiracy/conversion of classified documents, procurement fraud, and mail fraud.[35] In one 1992 incident, GE pled guilty to defrauding the Pentagon and agreed to pay $69 million in fines. The company took responsibility for the behavior of a former marketing employee who, working with an Israeli Air Force general, helped divert Pentagon funds to their personal bank accounts and to Israeli military programs that were unauthorized by the United States. As a result of these and other incidents (and being shut out of government contracts for six months), General Electric now strives to prevent isolated groups from hatching unethical or fraudulent plots.[36]

Once an organization has identified its "ethics sinkholes," it needs to promote ethical values within these areas. These values need to be communicated to key individuals, particularly those with access and control over information and staff; administrative assistants, for example, are often described as being among the most powerful people in organizations.[37] Communicating desired values to these employees and finding ways to make those values "stick" will provide the biggest payoff in terms of reforming the organization's informal culture.

Changing Society

In this book, drawing on the emerging field of behavioral ethics, we have focused primarily on documenting the psychological reasons good people engage in bad behaviors. And up to this point in the chapter, we have suggested ways of improving human judgment and improving organizations, goals that are important components of the larger agenda of improving ethics across society. But structural changes at the societal level are also needed to create a more ethical society. As we documented in the previous chapter, special-interest groups are often strategically exploitative and have found ways to use our bounded ethicality against us. Rather than accepting the distortions of parties that oppose wise change, voters can and should educate themselves about the actual facts behind key issues and support politicians who are wise and brave enough to advocate ethical policies. In addition, we should support campaign finance reform legislation (and the politicians who pursue such measures) that would curb the undue influence of special-interest groups. Proposals that move toward the public financing of campaigns deserve our serious consideration, and politicians who support public financing deserve our backing.

We can also use the ideas in this book to help well-intentioned politicians generate and implement ideas that would push us toward becoming a more ethical and efficient society. Along these lines, psychologists and behavioral economists recently have begun to develop a novel strategy for coping with the imperfections of human judgment. Beginning with the knowledge that people act in predictably irrational ways, these theorists then structure choices to optimally account for biased decision making. The result: better, more ethical decisions. In their important book *Nudge*, Richard Thaler and Cass Sunstein have pushed scholars and organizational decision makers at all levels to develop ingenious ways of designing choice environments to avoid systematic pitfalls in decision making. This strategy can be used throughout society to promote more ethical, wiser decisions. Here, we suggest how some of the psychological concepts developed throughout this book could be used to lead citizens toward more ethical decisions.

Changing Defaults

In chapter 1, we referred to Johnson and Goldstein's cross-European organ donation study, which revealed that policy defaults are a tremendous factor in people's decisions. Specifically, countries that have opt-in organ donation policies, where the default is not to harvest people's organs without their prior consent, sacrifice thousands of lives in comparison to opt-out policies, where the default is organ harvesting. As you will recall, countries with opt-in policies had donor consent rates of 4.3 to 27.5 percent, while countries with opt-out policies had donor consent rates of 85.9 to more than 99.9 percent. In the United States, where opt-in policies result in low organ donation rates and needless deaths, lack of awareness of the power of defaults produces results that most citizens likely would consider unethical. Knowledge of the influence of policy defaults could be used to dramatically increase donation rates without changing the options available to citizens. Indeed, Thaler and Sunstein have offered tremendous documentation of the power to nudge people toward wiser behavior by changing the default.

It's not just that defaults matter; it's that they matter far more than most of us expect them to matter. Default settings for home electronics such as air conditioners, refrigerators, and computer monitors could all be required by law to have lower presets while still giving the user the same range of power, and computer printers could be required to have a default of printing in draft mode—a lower cost, less ink-intensive mode.[38]

Such regulations could be enacted without limiting anyone's options, lead to better and more ethical decisions, and in most cases, make consumers better off financially.

Structuring Information to Expose Value Trade-offs

When it comes to promoting ethical behavior, how governments communicate to their citizens also makes a difference. Most people would agree that it would be more ethical for us, as a society, to consume less fuel. However, though most of us appreciate fuel efficiency, we do not like higher gas taxes and gas prices. Making matters worse, fuel efficiency can be hard to measure and understand. In the 1970s, the U.S. Environmental Protection Agency started a program that required car manufacturers to place stickers on new cars that told potential buyers about the efficiency of the car in miles per gallon. This system seems to make a great deal of sense, and it's certainly far better than providing no information about fuel efficiency to buyers.

Unfortunately, the way in which this information is conveyed is not ideal. Researchers Rick Larrick and Jack Soll figured out that measuring fuel efficiency as miles per gallon leads consumers to systematically misinterpret the available information.[39] Larrick and Soll describe the "MPG illusion" as the common, false belief that the amount of gas a car consumes decreases linearly as a function of a car's MPG, when the actual relationship is curvilinear. That is, most of us intuitively and falsely think that we'll achieve the same or similar fuel savings by trading a 10 MPG car for a 15 MPG car as we would by trading a 20 MPG car for a 25 MPG car. In fact, if you do the arithmetic, the former will save much more fuel than the second, holding miles driven constant. Imagine, for example, that you own two cars, each of which you drive 10,000 miles per year. One gets 10 MPG, and the other gets 20 MPG. When you trade in the 10 MPG car for a 15 MPG car, you reduce your fuel usage from 1,000 gallons to 667 gallons, saving 333 gallons. In contrast, when you trade in the 20 MPG car for a 25 MPG car, you reduce your fuel usage from 500 gallons to 400 gallons, saving only 100 gallons. Clearly, getting the lowest-MPG cars, the old gas guzzlers, off the road should be a critical goal in our society, even if drivers don't replace the guzzlers with small hybrids.

Larrick and Soll suggest that we would be far better off as a society by requiring stickers on new cars to convey information in the form of gallons per mile (GPM) instead of MPG. While the difference sounds semantic, GPM likely would lead consumers to pay far more attention to fuel economy information. Why? Because fuel consumption does decrease linearly with GPM, thereby correcting the MPG illusion. And in a study run by Larrick and Soll, participants more accurately chose fuel-efficient cars when consumption was expressed as GPM than as MPG. Europe, Canada, and Australia have already moved to volume-over-distance measures such as GPM, but the United States, Japan, India, and other countries have yet to correct the MPG illusion.

Though interesting in its own right, the MPG story reveals that the salience and clarity of information can affect the tendency of people to use the information at their disposal. To push people toward more ethical use of fuel, we need to change the format in which data is presented.

Increasing the Importance of Future Concerns

In chapter 3, we described how the common tendency to discount the future can lead people to make decisions that harm the environment and leave burdens, such as the national debt, for future generations. Many policies that eliminate the imposition of unethical decisions on future generations require people to make a small current sacrifice in return for larger future benefits (or to avoid larger future harms). Often, these proposals fail because people overweight the immediate costs of implementation. For example, should we increase fuel taxes to reduce consumption of a product that contributes to global climate change? Most citizens agree that the United States needs to reduce its contribution to this problem, yet legislative efforts face stiff opposition; few voters are willing to seeing the price of gas jump by fifty cents a gallon or more. In this type of classic want/should conflict, we give too much weight to our dislike of current costs (higher gas prices) and underweight long-term implications (efficiency).

Max's work with Todd Rogers offers one lever policymakers can use to better calibrate citizens' weighing of costs and benefits: a concept we call "future lock-in."[40] We have found that people are more likely to choose according to the interests of their "should" selves when making decisions about the future than when making decisions that will be implemented immediately. In exchange for a slight delay in implementation, otherwise unappealing policies may be able to achieve large increases in support. The time delay persuades people to look beyond their emotional dislike of incurring the immediate costs of implementation.

In our study, we started by identifying five policies that people report feeling they *should* support but do not actually *want* to support. One was a policy that would limit the number of fish that could be caught by the fishing industry to reduce ocean overharvesting. Participants were told the policy would increase the price of fish, create job loss in the fishing industry, protect the fish population in the oceans, and extend the survival of the fishing industry to a sustainable level. Half of the participants were told the policy would go into effect as soon as possible, while the other half were told the policy would be implemented four years from now. Creating the four-year delay dramatically increased the policy's acceptability.

This type of future lock-in could be immensely useful for policymakers who are trying to bolster support for particular policies. Most citizens agree we need to do more to solve global environmental problems, yet most proposed initiatives face strong opposition due to the short-term costs. Slightly delaying implementation would allow people to listen to the part of themselves that *should* support a given policy rather than to the side of them that does not want to incur the costs. An additional benefit of delaying a policy's implementation is that it gives people time to prepare for the legislation's impact. For instance, passing gas taxes that go into effect in the future allows car owners to enjoy more years of value from the vehicles they currently own and gives auto manufacturers time to modify their plants to create the models that match the new legislation. By leveraging the benefits of the future lock-in effect, policymakers could increase the proportion of people who support wise reforms.

In addition, because future lock-in can be achieved through minor differences in language, it can be completely costless. Consider that many policies are intended to go into effect in the future, yet are communicated in language that evokes immediate, self-interested concerns. Our research shows that how the timing of a policy is framed can have a strong influence on its level of support. This time, we asked a national sample about how favorably they would view a new law that would increase the price of gas by fifty-three cents in two years, but which they would vote on in a few months. The same story was read by all:

> If passed, this policy would reduce gas consumption by increasing the price of a gallon of gas by fifty-three cents. In doing this, the policy would reduce U.S. contribution of carbon emissions into the atmosphere, which is one of the leading causes of global climate change. This policy would also reduce U.S. dependence on oil from foreign countries, especially the Middle East. This fifty-three-cent price increase in a gallon of gas would also make gas more expensive for Americans, and increase the costs of all forms of travel, especially driving. It would also probably cost jobs in the short term as the gas price increase would slow economic growth. This policy would be voted on early in 2007 and go into effect in 2009.

Half of the participants were then asked, "How strongly would you oppose or support this policy, which would go into effect two years in the future?" The other half was asked, "How strongly would you oppose or support this policy, which would be voted on by Congress as soon as possible?" Participants who read the version with the question that mentioned the delay in implementation were significantly more likely to vote for the policy than were participants who read the version that mentioned the imminent congressional vote. This was true despite the fact that both groups were presented with the same policy, which would be voted on by

Congress at the same time and with the same implementation date. Simply changing participants' focus on the time period affected the acceptability of the policy.

The examples in this section highlight the potential of defaults, saliency, and delayed implementation to create wise policies that can be passed. While one might question whether these strategies should be needed, the fact is that they are. Not only do we need to envision wise legislation, but we need to create policies that have a real chance of passing and succeeding in the real world.

Final Thoughts

We do not know what ethical challenges you are facing in your personal and professional life, nor do we know what your ethical values are. What we do know is that many people fall far short of their own standards. Applying the lens of behavioral ethics, we have tried to identify ways in which you and the groups to which you belong can see the ethical implications of your actions more clearly and make choices that better align with your values. At the individual level, you are well positioned to reach the ethical standards you would rely on with greater self-awareness. At the organizational level, leaders now should better understand how the decisions they make will affect the ethicality of their colleagues. At the societal level, innovative tools exist to help governments profoundly influence their citizens' ethical behavior for the better. In the end, we hope we have shown that each one of us, using the tools at our disposal, can contribute toward creating a more ethical world.

Notes

Readers can visit www.blindspots-ethics.com/references for clickable links to all online materials cited in the notes.

Chapter 1
The Gap between Intended and Actual Ethical Behavior

1. This comparative overestimation could be caused by overestimating one's own ethicality or underestimating that of others. The following article provides convincing evidence that the effect is caused by overestimating one's own ethicality: N. Epley and D. Dunning (2000), "Feeling 'Holier Than Thou': Are Self-Serving Assessments Produced by Errors in Self- or Social Prediction?" *Journal of Personality and Social Psychology* 79:861–75.

2. B. Steverman and D. Bogoslaw (2008, October 18), "The Financial Crisis Blame Game," *BusinessWeek*, retrieved from http://www.businessweek.com/investor/content/oct2008/pi20081017_950382.htm.

3. F. Dobbin and A. Kalev (2007), "The Architecture of Inclusion: Evidence from Corporate Diversity Programs," *Harvard Journal of Law & Gender* 30 (2): 279–301.

4. http://www.aspencbe.org/documents/ExecutiveSummaryMBAStudentAttitudes Report2008.pdf.

5. C. D. Batson, J. L. Kobrynowicz, H. Dinnerstein, C. Kampf, and A. D. Wilson (1997), "In a Very Different Voice: Unmasking Moral Hypocrisy," *Journal of Personality and Social Psychology* 72:1335–48.

6. P. Valdesolo and D. DeSteno (2007), "Moral Hypocrisy: Social Groups and the Flexibility of Virtue," *Psychological Science* 18:689–90.

7. Pew Center poll (1995), "People, the Press and Their Leaders," retrieved from http://www.pbs.org/wgbh/pages/frontline/shows/press/other/view.html.

8. Adapted from F. Gino and L. Pierce (2009), "The Abundance Effect: Unethical Behavior in the Presence of Wealth," *Organizational Behavior and Human Decision Processes* 109:142–55; M. Schweitzer, L. Ordóñez, and B. Douma (2004), "Goal Setting as a Motivator of Unethical Behavior," *Academy of Management Journal* 47:422–32; N. Mazar and D. Ariely (2006), "Dishonesty in Everyday Life and Its Policy Implications," *Journal of Public Policy and Marketing* 25:117–26.

9. Gino and Pierce 2009.

10. M. H. Bazerman and D. Chugh (2006), "Bounded Awareness: Focusing Failures in Negotiation," in *Negotiation Theory and Research*, ed. L. L. Thompson (New York: Psychology Press), 7–26.

11. P. Singer (2009), *The Life You Can Save: Acting Now to End World Poverty* (New York: Random House).

12. S. Milgram (1963), "Behavioral Study of Obedience," *Journal of Abnormal and Social Psychology* 67:371–78.

13. J. M. Burger (2009), "Replicating Milgram: Would People Still Obey Today?" *American Psychologist* 64:1–11.

14. BBC World Service (2010, March 17), "'Game of Death' French TV Show Sparks Controversy, retrieved from http://www.bbc.co.uk/worldservice/news/2010/03/100318 _game_of_death_et_sl.shtml.

15. P. Werhane, L. Hartman, B. Parmar, and Dennis Moberg (book in progress), *Social Construction, Mental Models, and the Problem of Obedience.*

16. See D. Vaughn (1996), *The Challenger Launch Decision: Risky Technology, Culture, and Deviance at NASA* (Chicago: University of Chicago Press), for an excellent overall analysis of this disaster.

17. Roger M. Boisjoly (2006, May 15), "Telecon Meeting (Ethical Decisions—Morton Thiokol and the Challenger Disaster)," Online Ethics Center for Engineering and Research, National Academy of Engineering, retrieved from http://www.onlineethics.org/ Topics/profpractice/ppessays/thiokolshuttle/shuttle_telecon.aspx.

18. Boisjoly 2006.

19. Boisjoly 2006.

20. Boisjoly 2006.

21. Irving Janis (1972), *Victims of Groupthink: A Psychological Study of Foreign-Policy Decisions and Fiascoes* (Boston: Houghton, Mifflin).

22. There are certainly situations in which moral rules lead to good decisions. Here we simply focus on the potential downside of moral rules.

23. M. H. Bazerman, J. Baron, and K. Shonk (2001), *You Can't Enlarge the Pie: Six Barriers to Effective Government* (New York: Basic Books).

24. M. Janofsky (2004, March 19), "Scalia Refusing to Take Himself Off Cheney Case," *New York Times*, A1.

25. M. R. Banaji (2004), "The Opposite of a Great Truth Is Also True: Homage of Koan #7," in *Perspectivism in Social Psychology: The Yin and Yang of Scientific Progress*, ed. J. T. Jost and M. R. Banaji (Washington, DC: American Psychological Association), 127–40.

26. A. S. Grove (2002), *Swimming Across: A Memoir* (New York: Grand Central).

27. A. L. McGill (1989), "Context Effects in Judgments of Causation," *Journal of Personality and Social Psychology* 57:189–200.

28. J. Greene (2011), *The Moral Brain and How to Use It* (New York: Penguin).

Chapter 2
Why Traditional Approaches to Ethics Won't Save You

1. Adapted from P. Foot (1978), "The Problem of Abortion and the Doctrine of the Double Effect," in *Virtues and Vices* (Oxford: Basil Blackwell); J. J. Thomson (2011), "Killing, Letting Die, and the Trolley Problem," *The Monist* 59:204–17; Greene 2011.

2. I. Kant (1964), *Groundwork of the Metaphysics of Morals*, trans. H. J. Paton (New York: Harper Torchbooks); Greene 2011.

3. Greene 2011; F. A. Cushman (2008), "Crime and Punishment: Distinguishing the Roles of Causal and Intentional Analyses in Moral Judgment," *Cognition* 108 (2): 353–80.

4. Adapted from Foot 1978; Thomson 2011; Greene 2011.

5. Greene 2011.

6. M. C. Nussbaum (1997), *Cultivating Humanity: A Classical Defense of Reform in Liberal Education* (Cambridge: Harvard University Press); M. C. Nussbaum (2007), "Liberty of Conscience: The Attack on Equal Respect," *Journal of Human Development* 8:337–58; M. Moody-Adams (1997), *Fieldwork in Familiar Places: Morality, Culture, and Philosophy* (Cambridge: Harvard University Press).

7. R. A. Posner (1997), "Against Ethical Criticism," *Philosophy and Literature* 21 (1): 1–27.

8. E. Schwitzgebel (2009a), "Do Ethicists Steal More Books?" *Philosophical Psychology* 22:711–25.

9. E. Schwitzgebel and J. Rust (forthcoming), "Do Ethicists and Political Philosophers Vote More Often Than Other Professors?" *Review of Philosophy and Psychology*; E. Schwitzgebel and J. Rust (forthcoming), "The Moral Behavior of Ethicists: Peer Opinion," *Mind*.

10. E. Schwitzgebel (2009b, August 8), "Are Ethicists Ethical?" *The Philosopher's Zone*, audio interview, retrieved from http://www.abc.net.au/rn/philosopherszone/stories/2009/2645717.htm.

11. Schwitzgebel 2009a.

12. J. R. Rest (1986), *Moral Development: Advances in Research and Theory* (New York: Praeger).

13. A. E. Tenbrunsel and D. M. Messick (2004), "Ethical Fading: The Role of Self Deception in Unethical Behavior," *Social Justice Research* 17:223–36.

14. A. Speer (1970), *Inside the Third Reich*, trans. R. Winston and C. Winston (London: Weidenfeld and Nicolson).

15. J. Haidt, S. Koller, and M. Dias (1993), "Affect, Culture, and Morality, or, Is It Wrong to Eat Your Dog?" *Journal of Personality and Social Psychology* 65:613–28.

16. J. Haidt (2001), "The Emotional Dog and Its Rational Tail: A Social Intuitionist Approach to Moral Judgment," *Psychological Review* 108:814–34.

17. Haidt 2001.

18. J. Greene and J. Haidt (2002), "How (and Where) Does Moral Judgment Work?" *Trends in Cognitive Sciences* 6 (12):517–23.

19. K. A. Appiah (2007, December 9), "The New New Philosophy," *New York Times*, retrieved from http://www.nytimes.com/2007/12/09/magazine/09wwln-idealab -t.html?pagewanted=1&_r=1.

20. Appiah 2007.

21. K. E. Stanovich and R. F. West (2000), "Individual Differences in Reasoning: Implications for the Rationality Debate," *Behavioral & Brain Sciences* 23:645–65.

22. D. Kahneman (2003), "A Perspective on Judgment and Choice: Mapping Bounded Rationality," *American Psychologist* 58:697–720.

23. D. Chugh (2004), "Why Milliseconds Matter: Societal and Managerial Implications of Implicit Social Cognition," *Social Justice Research* 17:203–22.

24. N. Mead, R. F. Baumeister, F. Gino, M. Schweitzer, and D. Ariely (2009), "Too Tired to Tell the Truth: Self-Control Resource Depletion and Dishonesty," *Journal of Experimental Social Psychology* 45:594–97.

25. M. Kern and D. Chugh (2009), "Bounded Ethicality: The Perils of Loss Framing," *Psychological Science* 20:378–84.

26. D. T. Miller and R. K. Ratner (1998), "The Disparity between the Actual and Assumed Power of Self-Interest," *Journal of Personality and Social Psychology* 74:53–62.

Chapter 3
When We Act against Our Own Ethical Values

1. J. S. Cohen, S. St. Clair, and T. Malone (2009, May 29), "Clout Goes to College," *Chicago Tribune*, 1.

2. Cohen, St. Clair, and Malone 2009.

3. Cohen, St. Clair, and Malone 2009.

4. Cohen, St. Clair, and Malone 2009.

5. S. Saulny (2009, August 7), "U. of Illinois Manipulated Admissions, Panel Finds," *New York Times*, A10.

6. Cohen, St. Clair, and Malone 2009.

7. Cohen, St. Clair, and Malone 2009.

8. P. Schmidt (2007, April 6), "Children of Alumni Are Uniquely Harmed by Admissions Preferences, Study Finds," *Chronicle of Higher Education*.

9. "The Curse of Nepotism" (2004, January 8), *The Economist*.

10. "The Curse of Nepotism" 2004.

11. P. E. Tetlock, G. Mitchell, and T. L. Murray (2008), "The Challenge of Debiasing Personnel Decisions: Avoiding Both Under- and Overcorrection," *Industrial and Organizational Psychology* 1:439–43.

12. L. A. Rudman and R. D. Ashmore (2007), "Discrimination and the Implicit Association Test," *Group Processes and Intergroup Relations* 10 (3): 359–72.

13. M. Bertrand, D. Chugh, and S. Mullainathan (2005), "Implicit Discrimination," *American Economic Review* 95:94–98.

14. A. R. Green, D. R. Carney, D. J. Pallin, L. H. Ngo, K. L. Raymond, L. I. Lezzoni, and M. R. Banaji (2007), "Implicit Bias among Physicians and Its Prediction of Thrombolysis Decisions for Black and White Patients," *Journal of General Internal Medicine* 22:1231–38.

15. D. O. Rooth (2007), "Implicit Discrimination in Hiring: Real World Evidence," University of Kalmar, Institute for the Study of Labor (IZA) Discussion Paper No. 2764, Bonn, Germany.

16. J. Correll, B. Park, C. M. Judd, and B. Wittenbrink (2002), "The Police Officer's Dilemma: Using Ethnicity to Disambiguate Potentially Threatening Individuals," *Journal of Personality and Social Psychology* 83:1314–29.

17. C. Y. Johnson (2009, July 30), "Research Shows Key Role for Unconscious Bias; Attitudes Believed to Be Learned Early," *Boston Globe*, 4.

18. Johnson 2009.

19. S. Harris (1946), *Banting's Miracle: The Story of the Discovery of Insulin* (Toronto: J. M. Dent and Sons).

20. D. M. Messick and K. P. Sentis (1979), "Fairness and Preference," *Journal of Experimental Social Psychology* 15:418–34; D. M. Messick and K. P. Sentis (1983), "Fairness, Preference, and Fairness Biases," in *Equity Theory: Psychological and Sociological Perspectives*, ed. D. M. Messick and K. S. Cook (New York: Praeger), 61–94.

21. L. Thompson and G. Loewenstein (1992), "Egocentric Interpretations of Fairness and Interpersonal Conflict," *Organizational Behavior and Human Decision Processes* 51:176–97.

22. M. H. Bazerman and M. A. Neale (1982), "Improving Negotiation Effectiveness under Final Offer Arbitration: The Role of Selection and Training," *Journal of Applied Psychology* 67:543–48.

23. L. Babcock, G. Loewenstein, S. Issacharoff, and C. Camerer (1995), "Biased Judgments of Fairness in Bargaining," *American Economic Review* 85:1337–43.

24. E. Caruso, N. Epley, and M. H. Bazerman (2006), "The Costs and Benefits of Undoing Egocentric Responsibility Assessments in Groups," *Journal of Personality and Social Psychology* 9:857–71; L. R. Brawley (1984), "Unintentional Egocentric Biases in Attributions," *Journal of Sport Psychology* 6:264–78; D. R. Forsyth and B. R. Schlenker (1977), "Attributional Egocentrism Following Performance of a Competitive Task," *Journal of Social Psychology* 102:215–22; and A. Zander (1971), *Motives and Goals in Groups* (New York: Academic Press).

25. M. Ross and F. Sicoly (1979), "Egocentric Biases in Availability and Attribution," *Journal of Personality and Social Psychology* 37:322–36.

26. K. Bradsher (2009, July 15), "U.S. Officials Press China on Climate," *New York Times*, retrieved from http://www.nytimes.com/2009/07/16/world/asia/16warming.html.

27. "Managed to Death," (2008, October 30), editorial, *The Economist*.

28. "Managed to Death" 2008.

29. "Managed to Death" 2008.

30. "Managed to Death" 2008.

31. "Changing Tides: Banning the Trade in Bluefin Tuna" (2009, November 19), *The Economist*.

32. Bazerman, Baron, and Shonk 2001, 131–32.

33. K. A. Wade-Benzoni, A. E. Tenbrunsel, and M. H. Bazerman (1996), "Egocentric Interpretations of Fairness in Asymmetric, Environmental Social Dilemmas: Explaining Harvesting Behavior and the Role of Communication," *Organizational Behavior and Human Decision Processes* 67:111–26.

34. L. Babcock and G. Loewenstein (1997), "Explaining Bargaining Impasse: The Role of Self-Serving Biases," *Journal of Economic Perspectives* 11:109–26.

35. G. Loewenstein and R. H. Thaler (1989), "Anomalies: Intertemporal Choice," *Journal of Economic Perspectives* 3:181–93.

36. D. I. Laibson, A. Repetto, and J. Tobacman (1998), "Self-Control and Saving for Retirement," *Brookings Papers on Economic Activity* 1:91–196.

37. Bazerman, Baron, and Shonk 2001.

38. A. Gore (1992), *Earth in the Balance* (New York: Penguin).

39. K. A. Wade-Benzoni (1999), "Thinking about the Future: An Intergenerational Perspective on the Conflict and Compatibility between Economic and Environmental Interests," *American Behavioral Scientist* 42:1393–1405.

Chapter 4
Why You Aren't as Ethical as You Think You Are

1. Josephson Institute (2008), "Report Card on the Ethics of American Youth," retrieved from http://charactercounts.org/programs/reportcard/.

2. A. E. Tenbrunsel, K. A. Diekmann, K. A. Wade-Benzoni, and M. H. Bazerman (2011), "Why We Aren't as Ethical as We Think We Are: A Temporal Explanation," in *Research in Organizational Behavior*, ed. B. M. Staw and A. Brief, forthcoming.

3. J. A. Woodzicka and M. LaFrance (2001), "Real versus Imagined Gender Harassment," *Journal of Social Issues* 57 (1): 15–30.

4. T. M. Osberg and J. S. Shrauger (1986), "Self-Prediction: Exploring the Parameters

of Accuracy," *Journal of Personality and Social Psychology* 51:1044–57; K. A. Diekmann, A. E. Tenbrunsel, and A. D. Galinsky (2003), "From Self-Prediction to Self-Defeat: Behavioral Forecasting, Self-Fulfilling Prophecies, and the Effect of Competitive Expectations," *Journal of Personality and Social Psychology* 85:672–83.

5. M. H. Bazerman, A. E. Tenbrunsel, and K. Wade-Benzoni (1998), "Negotiating with Yourself and Losing: Making Decisions with Competing Internal Preferences," *Academy of Management Review* 23 (2): 225–41.

6. K. L. Milkman, T. Rogers, and M. H. Bazerman (2009), "Highbrow Films Gather Dust: Time-Inconsistent Preferences and Online DVD Rentals," *Management Science* 55:1047–59.

7. Epley and Dunning 2000.

8. Diekmann, Tenbrunsel, and Galinsky 2003.

9. Tenbrunsel and Messick 2004.

10. Rest 1986.

11. G. Loewenstein (1996), "Out of Control: Visceral Influences on Behavior," *Organizational Behavior and Human Decision Processes* 65:272–92.

12. C. Zhong and K. Liljenquist (2006), "Washing Away Your Sins: Threatened Morality and Physical Cleansing," *Science* 313 (5792): 1451–52.

13. Tenbrunsel et al. 2011.

14. N. Paharia and R. Deshpandé (2009), "Sweatshop Labor Is Wrong Unless the Jeans Are Cute: Motivated Moral Disengagement," Harvard Business School Working Paper No. 09-079.

15. L. Shu, F. Gino, and M. H. Bazerman (2010), "Dishonest Deed, Clear Conscience: When Cheating Leads to Moral Disengagement and Motivated Forgetting," forthcoming in *Personality and Social Psychology Bulletin.*

16. A. E. Tenbrunsel (1998), "Misrepresentation and Expectations of Misrepresentation in an Ethical Dilemma: The Role of Incentives and Temptation," *Academy of Management Journal* 41:330–39.

17. M. J. Osofsky, A. Bandura, and P. G. Zimbardo (2005), "The Role of Moral Disengagement in the Execution Process," *Law and Human Behavior* 29 (4): 371–93.

Chapter 5
When We Ignore Unethical Behavior

1. J. Swanson (2008, October 23), "Ratings Agencies Hit for Role in Financial Crisis," *MND Newswire*, retrieved from http://www.mortgagenewsdaily.com/10232008_Ratings_Agencies_.asp.

2. U. Neisser (1979), "The Concept of Intelligence," *Intelligence* 3 (3): 217–27.

3. *The Reader*, 2008, written by David Hare.

4. D. A. Moore, L. Tanlu, and M. H. Bazerman (2010), "Conflict of Interest and the Intrusion of Bias," *Judgment and Decision Making* 5 (1): 37–53.

5. Babcock and Loewenstein 1997.

6. T. Farragher (2002, December 14), "Admission of Awareness Damning for Law," *Boston Globe*, retrieved from http://www.boston.com/globe/spotlight/abuse/stories3/121402_admission.htm.

7. A. Berenson (2006, March 12), "A Cancer Drug's Big Price Rise Disturbs Doctors and Patients," *New York Times*, retrieved from http://www.nytimes.com/2006/03/12/business/worldbusiness/12iht-web.0312berenson.html?scp=2&sq=Berenson,%20A.%20%282006,%20March%2012%29.%20A%20Cancer%20Drug%27s%20Big%20Price%20Rise%20Disturbs%20Doctors%20and%20Patients&st=cse.

8. N. Paharia, K. S. Kassam, J. D. Greene, and M. H. Bazerman (2009), "Dirty Work, Clean Hands: The Moral Psychology of Indirect Agency," *Organizational Behavior and Human Decision Processes* 109:134–41.

9. Paharia et al. 2009.

10. L. Coffman (2010), "Intermediation Reduces Punishment and Reward," working paper.

11. "Belichick Fined" (2007, September 14), *Mike and Mike in the Morning*, ESPN.com audio podcast.

12. F. Gino and M. H. Bazerman (2009), "When Misconduct Goes Unnoticed: The Acceptability of Gradual Erosion in Others' Unethical Behavior," *Journal of Experimental Social Psychology* 45:708–19.

13. Tenbrunsel and Messick 2004; Gino and Bazerman 2009.

14. Gino and Bazerman 2009.

15. D. J. Simons (2000), "Current Approaches to Change Blindness," *Visual Cognition* 7 (1–3): 1–15.

16. F. Gino, D. A. Moore, and M. H. Bazerman (2010), "No Harm, No Foul: The Outcome Bias in Ethical Judgments," Harvard Business School Working Paper No. 08-080.

17. J. Baron and J. C. Hershey (1988), "Outcome Bias in Decision Evaluation," *Journal of Personality and Social Psychology* 54:569–79.

18. Gino, Moore, and Bazerman 2010.

19. F. A. Cushman, A. Dreber, Y. Wang, and J. Costa (2009), "Accidental Outcomes Guide Punishment in a 'Trembling Hand' Game," *PLOS One* 4 (8): e6699.

20. D. Moore, P. Tetlock, L. Tanlu, and M. H. Bazerman (2006), "Conflicts of Interest and the Case of Auditor Independence: Moral Seduction and Strategic Issue Cycling," *Academy of Management Review* 31 (1): 1–20.

21. M. H. Bazerman and M. D. Watkins (2004), *Predictable Surprises: The Disasters You Should Have Seen Coming and How to Prevent Them* (Boston: Harvard Business School Press).

22. A. Levitt and P. Dwyer (2002), *Take on the Street: What Wall Street & Corporate America Don't Want You to Know* (New York: Pantheon); J. Berardino (2000), Managing Partner, Arthur Andersen LLP, Testimony before the SEC Public Hearings on Auditor Independence, Washington, DC, http://www.sec.gov/rules/extra/audmin.htm; *United States v. Arthur Young & Co.*, 465 U.S. 805 (1984); Moore at al. 2006.

23. D. A. Small and G. Loewenstein (2003), "Helping a Victim or Helping the Victim: Altruism and Identifiability," *Journal of Risk and Uncertainty* 26 (1): 5–16; D. A. Small and G. Loewenstein (2005), "The Devil You Know: The Effects of Identifiability on Punitiveness," *Journal of Behavioral Decision Making* 18:311–18; T. Kogut and I. Ritov (2005), "The 'Identified Victim' Effect: An Identified Group or Just a Single Individual?" *Journal of Behavioral Decision Making* 18:157–67; T. Kogut and I. Ritov (2005), "The Singularity Effect of Identified Victims in Separate and Joint Evaluation," *Organizational Behavior and Human Decision Processes* 97:106–16.

24. Small and Loewenstein 2003.

25. J. Chatzky (2004, February), "Meet the Whistle-Blower," *Money*, retrieved from http://money.cnn.com/pr/subs/magazine_archive/2004/02/MTK.html.

26. Chatzky 2004.

27. Chatzky 2004.

Chapter 6
Placing False Hope in the "Ethical Organization"

1. A. VanderMey (2009, June 11), "Harvard's MBA Oath Goes Viral," *Business-Week*, retrieved from http://www.businessweek.com/bschools/content/jun2009/bs20090611_522427.htm.

2. From http://mbaoath.org.

3. H. Hurt III (2005, May 15), "Drop That Ledger! This Is the Compliance Officer," *New York Times*, retrieved from http://www.nytimes.com/2005/05/15/business/yourmoney/15comply.html?_r=1&pagewanted=2&sq=compliance&st=cse&scp=6.

4. W. C. Rhoden (2009, April 10), "University Compliance Officers: Good Cop, Bad Cop," *New York Times*, retrieved from http://www.nytimes.com/2009/04/11/sports/ncaabasketball/11rhoden.html?scp=2&sq=compliance&st=cse.

5. Hurt 2005.

6. A. E. Tenbrunsel, K. Smith-Crowe, and E. E. Umphress (2003), "Building Houses on Rocks: The Role of Ethical Infrastructure in the Ethical Effectiveness of Organizations," *Social Justice Research* 16:285–307.

7. L. D. Ordóñez, M. E. Schweitzer, A. D. Galinsky, and M. H. Bazerman (2009), "On Good Scholarship, Goal Setting, and Scholars Gone Wild," *Academy of Management Perspectives* 23 (3): 82–87.

8. P. Coy (2008, February 27), "Bill Clinton's Drive to Increase Homeownership Went Way Too Far," *BusinessWeek*, retrieved from http://www.businessweek.com/the_thread/hotproperty/archives/2008/02/clintons_drive.html.

9. C. Drew (2009, April 2), "Military Contractor Agrees to Pay $325 Million to Settle Whistle-Blower Lawsuit," *New York Times*, retrieved from http://www.nytimes.com/2009/04/03/business/03whistle.html?_r=1&scp=5&sq=northrop%20gumman%20and%20false%20claims%20act&st=cse.

10. S. Kerr (1975), "On the Folly of Rewarding A, While Hoping for B," *Academy of Management Journal* 18:769–83.

11. M. Santoro and L. Paine (1993), "Sears Auto Centers," Harvard Business School Case 9-394-010.

12. B. M. Staw and R. D. Boettger (1990), "Task Revision: A Neglected Form of Work Performance," *Academy of Management Journal* 33:534–59.

13. "Obama's Health Care Speech to Congress" (2009, September 9), *New York Times*, retrieved from http://www.nytimes.com/2009/09/10/us/politics/10obama.text.html?pagewanted=1&_r=1.

14. Ongoing field research by Ann Tenbrunsel.

15. M. Cheng, K. R. Subramanyam, and Y. Zhang (2005), "Earnings Guidance and Managerial Myopia," working paper, University of Southern California.

16. D. Henry (2009, August 4), "SEC Fines GE $50 Million for Accounting Misdeeds,"

BusinessWeek, retrieved from http://www.businessweek.com/bwdaily/dnflash/content/aug2009/db2009084_567813.htm.

17. A. E. Tenbrunsel and D. M. Messick, (1999), "Sanctioning Systems, Decision Frames and Cooperation Journal," *Administrative Science Quarterly* 44:684–707.

18. U. Gneezy and A. Rustichini (2000), "A Fine Is a Price," *Journal of Legal Studies* 29 (1): 1–17.

19. Tenbrunsel and Messick 1999.

20. J. W. Brehm (1966), *A Theory of Psychological Reactance* (Oxford: Academic Press).

21. F. Gino, S. Ayal, and D. Ariely (2010), "Altruistic Cheating: Behaving Dishonestly for the Sake of Others," working paper.

22. U. Khan and R. Dhar (2006), "Licensing Effect in Consumer Choice," *Journal of Marketing Research* 43 (2): 259–66; A. H. Jordan and B. Monin (2008), "From Sucker to Saint: Moralization in Response to Self-Threat," *Psychological Science* 19:809–15; B. Monin and D. T. Miller (2001), "Moral Credentials and the Expression of Prejudice," *Journal of Personality and Social Psychology* 81:33–43.

23. S. Sachdeva, R. Iliev, and D. L. Medin (2009), "Sinning Saints and Saintly Sinners: The Paradox of Moral Self-Regulation," *Psychological Science* 20:523–28.

24. J. M. Carlsmith and A. E. Gross (1969), "Some Effects of Guilt on Compliance," *Journal of Personality and Social Psychology* 11:232–39.

25. J. Jordan, F. Gino, M. C. Leliveld, and A. E. Tenbrunsel (2010), "Moral Compensation and the Environment: Affecting Individuals' Moral Intentions through How They See Themselves as Moral," working paper, University of Groningen.

26. D. Cain, G. Loewenstein, and D. Moore (2005), "The Dirt on Coming Clean: Perverse Effects of Disclosing Conflicts of Interest," *Journal of Legal Studies* 34 (1): 1–25.

27. Tenbrunsel, Smith-Crowe, and Umphress 2003, 288.

28. P. Selznick (1948), "Foundations of the Theory of Organization," *American Sociological Review* 13:25–35; E. E. Lawler and J. G. Rhode (1976), *Information and Control in Organizations* (Tucson: Good Year).

29. In the interest of full disclosure: Johnson & Johnson has been a regular client of Max's for more than twenty years.

30. R. Susi (2002), "Effective Crisis Management," retrieved from http://iml.jou.ufl.edu/projects/Fall02/Susi/tylenol.htm.

31. Tenbrunsel, Smith-Crowe, and Umphress 2003.

32. "High-Powered Business Leaders Praise Corporate Cleanup Law" (2003, October 3), retrieved from Nationaljournal.com, http://www.nationaljournal.com/congressdaily/dj_20031003_7a.php ?mrefid=site_search.

33. A. C. Hollinger and J. P. Clark (1983), *Theft by Employees* (New York: Lexington Books).

34. W. H. Redmond (2008), "Formal Institutions in Historical Perspective," *Journal of Economic Issues* 42:569–76.

35. D. C. North (1990), *Institutions, Institutional Change, and Economic Performance* (Cambridge: Cambridge University Press).

36. T. Loughran, B. McDonald, and H. Yun (2008), "A Wolf in Sheep's Clothing: The Use of Ethics-Related Terms in 10-K Reports," *Journal of Business Ethics* 89 (1): 39–49.

37. M. Forster, T. Loughran, and B. McDonald (2008), "Commonality in Codes of Ethics," working paper, University of Notre Dame.

38. F. McRoberts (2002, September 1), "A Final Accounting: The Fall of Andersen," *Chicago Tribune*, retrieved from http://www.chicagotribune.com/news/chi-0209010315 sep01,0,538751.story.

39. B. L. Toffler and J. Reingold (2003), *Final Accounting: Greed, Ambition, and the Fall of Arthur Andersen* (New York: Broadway Business), 124.

40. A. Barrioneuvo (2006, May 3), "Hostility May Cost Ken Lay," *New York Times*, retrieved from http://query.nytimes.com/gst/fullpage.html?res=9404E4DE1E3FF930A3575 6C0A9609C8B63.

41. G. Carlin (1990), "They're Only Words," track 14 on *Parental Advisory: Explicit Lyrics* (CD), Atlantic/Wea.

42. D. Barstow and L. Bergman (2003, January 9), "A Family's Fortune, a Legacy of Blood and Tears," *New York Times*, retrieved from http://www.nytimes.com/2003/01/09/ us/a-family-s-fortune-a-legacy-of-blood-and-tears.html?scp=5&sq=disguising+behavior+thr ough+words&st=nyt.

43. R. Worthington (1993, October 15), "Whistleblower Slain after Police Release Tape of His Call," *Chicago Tribune*, retrieved from http://community.seattletimes.nwsource.com/ archive/?date=19931015&slug=1726192.

44. J. Werdigier (2009, November 9), "Financial Regulations Chief Chides British Banks," *New York Times*, retrieved from http://www.nytimes.com/2009/11/10/business/ global/10fsa.html?_r=1&scp=10&sq=bonusses%20and%20risky%20behavior&st=cse.

Chapter 7
Why We Fail to Fix Our Corrupted Institutions

1. R. N. Proctor (2001), "Tobacco and the Global Lung Cancer Epidemic," *Nature Review* 1 (1): 82–86.

2. Proctor 2001.

3. A. M. Brandt (2007), *The Cigarette Century* (New York: Basic Books).

4. J. Stiglitz (1998), "The Private Uses of Public Interests: Incentives and Institutions," *Journal of Economic Perspectives* 12:3–22.

5. Stiglitz 1998.

6. There may be good deontological reasons to depart from this utilitarian logic in some cases. But, generally, this utilitarian approach would create greater good for society.

7. Bazerman, Baron, and Shonk 2001.

8. Proctor 2001.

9. Proctor 2001; Brandt 2007.

10. Proctor 2001.

11. Proctor 2001; Brandt 2007.

12. Brandt 2007.

13. D. Pearson and J. Anderson (1968), *The Case against Congress: A Compelling Indictment of Corruption on Capitol Hill* (New York: Simon and Schuster), 360–61.

14. Brandt 2007.

15. Graham, E. A. (1954), foreword to *Smoking and Cancer*, by Alton Ochsner (New York: Meissner), vii–viii.

16. Brandt 2007.

17. M. H. Bazerman, K. Morgan, and G. F. Loewenstein (1997, Summer), "The Impossibility of Auditor Independence," *Sloan Management Review* 38 (4): 89–94.

18. Smith, H. (2002, March 12), "Bigger Than Enron: Interview with Arthur Levitt," *Frontline*, PBS.

19. Mayer, J. (2010, April 22–29), "The Accountants' War," *New Yorker*, 70.

20. Lay, K. (2000, September 20), "Letter to Arthur Levitt," in "Bigger Than Enron: Letter from Kenneth Lay," *Frontline*, PBS, retrieved from http://www.pbs.org/wgbh/pages/frontline/shows/regulation/congress/lay.html.

21. Smith, H. (2002), "Bigger Than Enron: Comment on Letter from Kenneth Lay," *Frontline*, PBS, retrieved from http://www.pbs.org/wgbh/pages/frontline/shows/regulation/congress/.

22. Bazerman and Watkins 2004, 50.

23. The Center for Responsive Politics is a nonpartisan, nonprofit Washington, DC, research group that tracks money in politics. Data are available at www.opensecrets.org.

24. Bazerman, Morgan, and Loewenstein 1997, 90.

25. M. H. Bazerman, G. F. Loewenstein, and D. Moore (2002, November), "Why Good Accountants Do Bad Audits," *Harvard Business Review*, 97–102.

26. F. Norris (2000, July 27), "3 Big Accounting Firms Assail SEC's Proposed Restrictions," *New York Times*, C9.

27. Norris 2000, C9.

28. J. Berardino (2000, July 26), transcript, U.S. Securities & Exchange Commission Hearing on Auditor Independence, http://www.sec.gov/rules/extra/audmin.htm.

29. Mayer 2010, 70.

30. Mayer 2010, 70.

31. Mayer 2010, 70.

32. Mayer 2010, 66.

33. Cain, Loewenstein, and Moore 2005.

34. P. Krugman (2009, December 27), "The Big Zero," *New York Times*, retrieved from http://www.nytimes.com/2009/12/28/opinion/28krugman.html?em.

35. M. J. de la Merced (2010, March 12), "Findings on Lehman Take Even Experts by Surprise," *New York Times*, retrieved from http://www.nytimes.com/2010/03/13/business/13lehman.html?scp=1&sq=lehman%2C+ernst&st=nyt.

36. O. Zill de Granados (2007), "The Doubters of Global Warming," *Frontline*, PBS, retrieved from http://www.pbs.org/wgbh/pages/frontline/hotpolitics/reports/skeptics.html.

37. Union of Concerned Scientists (2007, January), *Smoke, Mirrors and Hot Air: How ExxonMobil Uses Big Tobacco's Tactics to Manufacture Uncertainty on Climate Science*, retrieved from http://www.ucsusa.org/assets/documents/global_warming/exxon_report.pdf.

38. Zill de Granados 2007.

39. Union of Concerned Scientists 2007.

40. I. Sample (2007, February 2), "Scientists Offered Cash to Dispute Climate Study," *The Guardian*, retrieved from http://www.guardian.co.uk/environment/2007/feb/02/frontpagenews.climatechange.

41. J. Donnelly (2007, February 15), "Debate over Global Warming Is Shifting," *Boston Globe*, retrieved from http://www.boston.com/news/nation/washington/articles/2007/02/15/debate_over_global_warming_is_shifting/.

42. Watson et al. 2001. The *Third Assessment Report* of the Intergovernmental Panel

on Climate Change presents a comprehensive overview of the consequences of climate change; retrieved from http://www.grida.no/publications/other/ipcc_tar/.

43. Watson et al. 2001.

44. J. M. Broder and E. Rosenthal (2009, December 17), "Obama Has Goal to Wrest a Deal in Climate Talks," *New York Times*, retrieved from http://www.nytimes.com/2009/12/18/science/earth/18climate.html.

45. M. H. Bazerman (2006), "Climate Change as a Predictable Surprise," *Climatic Change* 77 (1–2): 1–15.

46. L. Lessig (2009, October 8), "Setting the Framework for the Question of Institutional Corruption," recorded lecture, Kennedy School of Government, Harvard University, retrieved from http://www.ethics.harvard.edu/news-and-events/lectures-and-events.

47. W. Samuelson and R. J. Zeckhauser (1988), "Status Quo Bias in Decision Making," *Journal of Risk and Uncertainty* 1 (1): 7–59.

48. D. Kahneman and A. Tversky (1982), "The Psychology of Preferences," *Scientific American* 246 (1): 160–73.

49. Samuelson and Zeckhauser 1988.

50. J. Y. Jost and M. R. Banaji (1994), "The Role of Stereotyping in System-Justification and the Production of False Consensus," *British Journal of Social Psychology* 33 (1): 1–27.

51. Brandt 2007.

52. Brandt 2007.

53. Brandt 2007.

54. This problem was first presented in M. H. Bazerman, D. A. Moore, P. E. Tetlock, and L. Tanlu (2006), "Reports of Solving the Conflicts of Interest in Auditing Are Highly Exaggerated," *Academy of Management Review* 31:1–7.

55. Of course, there have been some courageous exceptions. For example, in 1997 Lord John Browne, then the CEO of British Petroleum, made clear that he believed climate change existed and was caused by human actions, but this was years after a clear scientific consensus had emerged on the issue.

Chapter 8
Narrowing the Gap: Interventions for Improving Ethical Behavior

1. J. S. Hammond, R. L. Keeney, and H. Raiffa (1999), *Smart Choices* (Boston: Harvard Business School Press).

2. M. H. Bazerman and M. R. Banaji (2004), "The Social Psychology of Ordinary Unethical Behavior," *Social Justice Research* 17:111–15.

3. D. Moore and G. F. Loewenstein (2004), "Self-Interest, Automaticity, and the Psychology of Conflict of Interest," *Social Justice Research* 17:189–202.

4. K. A. Diekmann, A. D. Galinsky, S. D. Sillito, and A. E. Tenbrunsel (2010), "An Examination of the Relationship between Behavioral Forecasts and Interpersonal Condemnation in Two Organizational Conflict Situations," working paper, University of Utah.

5. Y. Trope and N. Liberman (2003), "Temporal Construal," *Psychological Review* 110:403–21.

6. M. C. Gentile (2010), *Giving Voice to Values* (New Haven: Yale University Press).

7. Y. Trope and A. Fishbach (2000), "Counteractive Self-Control in Overcoming Temptation," *Journal of Personality and Social Psychology* 79:493–506; R. H. Strotz (1956), "Myopia

and Inconsistency in Dynamic Utility Maximization," *Review of Economic Studies* 23 (3): 165–80; R. H. Thaler and H. Shefrin (1981), "An Economic Theory of Self Control," *Journal of Political Economy* 89 (2): 392–406.

8. T. C. Schelling (1984), *Choice and Consequence: Perspectives of an Errant Economist* (Cambridge: Harvard University Press).

9. N. Ashraf, D. Karlan, and W. Yin (2006), "Tying Odysseus to the Mast: Evidence from a Commitment Savings Product in the Philippines," *Quarterly Journal of Economics* 121:635–72.

10. J. Brockner and J. Z. Rubin (1985), *Entrapment in Escalating Conflicts: A Social Psychological Analysis* (New York: Springer-Verlag); B. M. Staw and J. Ross (1987), "Behavior in Escalation Situations: Antecedents, Prototypes, and Solutions," in *Research in Organizational Behavior*, vol. 9, ed. L. L. Cummings and B. M. Staw (Greenwich, CT: JAI Press), 39–78.

11. Trope and Liberman 2003.

12. M. L. Rodriguez, W. Mischel, and Y. Shoda (1989), "Cognitive Person Variables in the Delay of Gratification of Older Children at Risk," *Journal of Personality and Social Psychology* 57:358–67.

13. Y. Shoda, W. Mischel, and P. K. Peake (1990), "Predicting Adolescent Cognitive and Self-Regulatory Competencies from Preschool Delay of Gratification: Identifying Diagnostic Conditions," *Developmental Psychology* 26:978–86.

14. W. Mischel (1996), "From Good Intentions to Willpower," in *The Psychology of Action: Linking Cognition and Motivation to Behavior*, ed. P. M. Gollwitzer and J. A. Bargh (New York: Guilford Press), 197–218.

15. Bazerman, Tenbrunsel, and Wade-Benzoni 1998.

16. J. R. Irwin, P. Slovic, S. Lichtenstein, and G. H. McClelland (1993), "Preference Reversals and the Measurement of Environmental Values," *Journal of Risk and Uncertainty* 6 (1): 5–18.

17. B. Fischhoff (1982), "Debiasing," in *Judgment under Uncertainty: Heuristics and Biases*, ed. D. Kahneman, P. Slovic, and A. Tversky (Cambridge: Cambridge University Press), 422–32; M. H. Bazerman and D. Moore (2008), *Judgment in Managerial Decision Making*, 7th ed. (Hoboken, NJ: John Wiley & Sons).

18. Tenbrunsel and Messick 2004.

19. R. P. Larrick (2004), "Debiasing," in *Blackwell Handbook of Judgment and Decision Making*, ed. D. J. Koehler and N. Harvey (Oxford: Blackwell), 316–37.

20. S. Lichtenstein and B. Fischhoff (1980), "Training for Calibration," *Organizational Behavior and Human Decision Processes* 26:149–71; Fischhoff 1982; Larrick 2004.

21. Larrick 2004; J. S. Lerner, and P. E. Tetlock (1999), "Accounting for the Effects of Accountability," *Psychological Bulletin* 125 (2): 255–75.

22. D. Birsch and J. H. Fielder (1994), *The Ford Pinto Case: A Study in Applied Ethics, Business, and Technology* (Albany: State University of New York Press), 19–21.

23. A. E. Tenbrunsel, K. Smith-Crowe, S. Chan-Serafin, E. E. Umphress, E. E. Brief, and J. Joseph (2010), "The Ethics 'Fix': When Formal Systems Make a Difference," working paper, University of Notre Dame.

24. The Engineer (2006, October 24), "Ford Pinto," Engineering.com, retrieved from http://www.engineering.com/Library/ArticlesPage/tabid/85/articleType/ArticleView/articleId/166/Ford-Pinto.aspx.

25. Toffler and Reingold 2003, 124.

26. Birsch and Fielder 1994, 23.

27. Birsch and Fielder 1994, 23.

28. C. D. Kerns (2003), "Why Good Leaders Do Bad Things: Mental Gymnastics behind Unethical Behavior," *Graziadio Business Report* 6 (4), retrieved from http://gbr.pepperdine.edu/034/leaders.html.

29. P. Rozin, M. Markwith, and B. Ross (1990), "The Sympathetic Magical Law of Similarity, Nominal Realism, and Neglect of Negatives in Response to Negative Labels," *Psychological Science* 1:383–84.

30. Bazerman, Tenbrunsel, and Wade-Benzoni 1998; Tenbrunsel and Messick 2004.

31. Bazerman, Tenbrunsel, and Wade-Benzoni 1998; S. Sonenshein (2007), "The Role of Construction, Intuition, and Justification in Responding to Ethical Issues at Work: The Sensemaking-Intuition Model," *Academy of Management Review* 32:1022–40.

32. Chugh 2004.

33. The Engineer 2006.

34. B. Shiv and A. Fedorikhin (1999), "Heart and Mind in Conflict: The Interplay of Affect and Cognition in Consumer Decision Making," *Journal of Consumer Research* 26 (3): 278–92.

35. C. Cray, "General Electric," *CorpWatch*, retrieved from http://www.corpwatch.org/section.php?id=16.

36. D. H. Blake (2008), interview, BGS Center for Ethical Business Leadership, retrieved from http://www.eblcenter.org/EBLTopics/ManagementToolsandPracticesforBusiness/tabid/471/VideoId/227/CategoryId/62/page/3/type/TopRated/62/language/en-US/Default.aspx/categoryId/62/language/en-US/Default.aspx.

37. D. Mechanic (1962), "Sources of Power of Lower Participants in Complex Organizations," *Administrative Science Quarterly* 7:349–64.

38. X. Gabaix and D. Laibson (2006), "Shrouded Attributes, Consumer Myopia, and Information Suppression in Competitive Markets," *Quarterly Journal of Economics* 121:505–40.

39. R. P. Larrick and J. Soll (2008), "The MPG Illusion," *Science* 320 (5883): 1593–94.

40. T. Rogers and M. H. Bazerman (2008), "Future Lock-in: Future Implementation Increases Selection of 'Should' Choices," *Organizational Behavioral and Human Decision Processes* 106:1–20.

Index